KW-054-002

1.00

смн

28/7

NORWAY

1 *Detail of the painted ceiling of the canopy in the stave church at Vik (see also plate 13)*

Barbara Øvstedal

NORWAY

B. T. Batsford Ltd
London

First published 1973
© Barbara Øvstedal 1973

0 7134 0177 X

Printed by Cox & Wyman Ltd, Fakenham
for the publishers
B. T. Batsford Ltd
4 Fitzhardinge Street, London W1

Contents

Note on spelling:

The letter ø can be written ö – Øvstedal, Røros *or* Röros; the letter A can be written Ålesund *or* Aalesund, Håkon *or* Haakon.

The Plates

9

Acknowledgments

My grateful thanks are due to: Professor Sverre Øvstedal; Professor Stein Tveite; Vervarslinga for Nord Norge; Northern Lights Observatory; Reiselivsforeningen i Molde; Turistkontorene i Oslo, Skien, og Kristiansand.

The author and publishers wish to thank the following for permission to reproduce photographs:

Norwegian State Railway for 6, 18, 20, 28; A. F. Kersting for 1–5, 7–9, 12–17, 19, 21, 23, 25, 27, 29–31; J. Allan Cash for 22, 24, 26 and Eric de la Maré for 10 and 11. Map by Patrick Leeson.

ARCTIC OCEAN

North Cape

Hammerfest

FINMARK

Kirkenes

Tromsø

U.S.S.R.

Kautokeino

FINLAND

Arctic Circle

Lofoten Is.

Svolvær

Narvik

SWEDEN

(CONTINUATION N.E. on same scale)

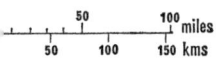

| 50 | | 100 | miles |
| 50 | 100 | 150 | kms |

NORWEGIAN SEA

SWEDEN

Trondheim

Ålesund

Andalsnes

Rorøs

Dombas

Lom

Lillehamar

Bergen

Rjukan

OSLO

Horten

Moss

Åsgårdstrand

Fredrikstad

Stavanger

Tønsberg

Bygland

Arendal

Kristiansand

Skagerrak

NORWAY

TO MY HUSBAND, INGE

1. Introduction

In full view of the passing traffic on the Road of the Ancients in Østfold there are rock carvings dating back 3,000 years, their location clearly marked by the Norwegian Tourist Association's blue and white sign that denotes sights of exceptional interest. The primitive, high-prowed longboats, forerunners of the Viking ships, sail for ever with their pin-men crews amid symbols and motifs of those dark, lost years. In one place a young hand and forearm must have been placed flat against the rock-face for that Bronze Age artist to tap around with his humble tools.

Throughout Norway there are over 15,000 of these rock carvings, and with the exception of a small percentage removed to museums they remain on stark mountainsides, by rivers, shaded by conifers, and spread out over smooth rocky substrata rising hump-shouldered out of the grass. It is a widespread exhibition of pre-historic art that stretches from the rolling hills of Østfold to far beyond the Arctic Circle in North Norway.

The earliest carvings from the Stone Age show the hunter's prey: elk, reindeer, stag and bear; sometimes whale, salmon, halibut, and occasionally seal, but all wonderfully shaped and often amazingly true to life. At Leiknes in Nordland a fine pair of elegant-necked swans can be seen. The later Bronze Age carvings, such as those on the Road of the Ancients, still show the hunter and the wild life he killed, but in addition there is the farmer with his cattle, horses and dogs, together with boats and carts, and many signs that indicate a land-wide worship of the sun. Skiers appear, but none is more clearly depicted than the 4,000-year-old rock carving found at Rødøy in North Norway, now in the ski-museum in Oslo, which shows unmistakably an experienced skier on long, well-shaped skis. Thus are the activities of sea, land and snow shown in their early beginnings, a pattern already set for a way of life that has evolved out of a constant struggle for survival since man first settled in Norway over 10,000 years ago.

Norway's shape is not unlike that of an ancient ski. The full curve of the south thins out into the 1,089 miles that make up the distance in a straight line from Lindenes to North Cape, only just over three miles across at its narrowest part and sliced through by the Arctic Circle where the ski-bindings would come. Yet its fjord-cleft, deeply indented coastline, warmed by the Gulf Stream that keeps ice from the harbours and temperatures up, is 17,000 miles long, jewelled by over 150,000 islands, quite apart from skerries without number. Out-lying Norwegian territories include Svalbard (Spitsbergen), Jan Mayen, Bear Island, Bouvet Island, and Peter I Island.

Norway is the fifth largest country in Europe, but its entire population still numbers less than four million. Over a third of it lies north of the 65th parallel, and as rugged mountains, high plateaux, glacier tables, thick forests and many lakes cover almost all the land area only 3·3 per cent of it is fit for cultivating. The gentle slopes to the east are irregularly balanced by the steep drops into the sea on the west, where spectacular fjords, cut by glaciers in the Ice Age and flooded by the sea when the great inland ice mass withdrew, penetrate as far as 114 miles inland. Most of them are comparatively shallow at the mouth, due to the lighter pressure of the ice cap on the coast, but in the interior the weight was so tremendous that the old river valleys were gouged to depths of 4,000 feet or more. Often the depth of water below the surface is equal to the height of the mountains rising above it.

Norway has more hours of light in summer than any other inhabited country. From mid May to the end of July the midnight sun bathes the North for twenty-four hours of the day, and keeps night at bay from the rest of the land. The very nature of the climate and terrain has resulted in a people uniquely homogeneous, and made them singularly hardy, independent and resolute, but never insular, their close link with the sea having ever turned their gaze outward beyond the 'North Way' that has been theirs alone for so long.

From the beginning of the eighth century the Viking ships went sweeping across the North Sea, and as the Norsemen's power and range increased in the ninth and tenth centuries the small agrarian communities at home became organized into larger governing and military regions. The Vikings – warriors and traders, plunderers and explorers, settlers and colonizers – voyaged as far as Byzantium, the Arab world, North Africa, Greenland, Iceland and North America. Early in the thirteenth century the Icelandic chronicler, Snorre Sturlasson, set down in his *Sagas of the Kings* the wars and feuds of the Vikings, their mythology, their belief that to fall in battle was to gain afterlife with Odin the Wise in Valhalla, and their certainty in the coming of Ragnarok, the final confrontation between Good and Evil. Runic script, an indigenous form of writing created to be carved rather than written, is to be found on the great rune-stones, the earliest dating from A.D. 200, many of which stand on their original sites and give additional information about the men who lived and died in Viking times.

The Vikings had their own rich culture, and in Norway itself there was a remarkably democratic system of administering law and order, in which free men met at certain meeting-places, known as Things, to hear grievances and settle civil disputes. This system of civil law was already centuries old in A.D. 872 when the young Viking king, Harald Fairhair, who had vowed not to cut his splendid mane of hair until all Norway was his, united the whole of the land for the first time into one realm under his supreme rule. His achievement was due in no small way to his love for a beautiful girl, Gyda, who had refused his offer of marriage, saying she would only be wife to the king of all Norway. He married his Gyda, and – in the Viking way – took other wives as well. He had many children, and through his line the state was moulded and strengthened, and the monarchy consolidated. One of his descendants was Olav

Tryggvason, the Viking king who introduced Christianity into Norway.

Another king of the House of Fairhair was Olav Haraldsson, who was destined to become the patron saint of Norway. Through him the Church was established, for following his heroic death in battle a great wave of conversion swept over the land, banishing Odin and the old gods for ever. He was declared a saint, and has been known as Olav the Holy ever since.

An old farmer in Nordfjord, whose land has been cultivated since Viking times, once said to me that when the Vikings turned their swords into ploughshares so did their strength decline. It is certainly true that less than 40 years after the death of Saint Olav the last great Viking king, Harald Hardråde (Hard-rule) was killed in the battle of Stamford Bridge in 1066, leaving the subjugation of England to William the Conqueror, who was himself a descendant of the Norwegian Viking, Rollo. When Harald Hardråde's grandson, Magnus, fell in battle in Ulster the Viking Age came to an end.

But the lust for fighting was still rampant, and the cleaving swords turned inwards, resulting in a bitterly troubled time of dynastic struggles and civil war until 1240. Then followed the quiet and prosperous reign of Håkon Håkonssøn, who held court at Bergen, which was the capital at that time. Surprisingly enough, throughout all the strife the traditional rights of free men remained, and in the 1270s under Magnus the Law-Mender a new common law for the whole kingdom was introduced, erasing the small differences that had existed in some areas.

But already troubles were brewing up again. Håkon v removed the court to Oslo, which has been the capital ever since, and when he died in 1319 he was succeeded by his Swedish grandson, who became Håkon vi, uniting Norway and Sweden under his rule. This was the fateful launching of Norway into 495 years as an overshadowed partner of Nordic unions, a state of affairs hastened by the devastating effect of the Black Death, which wiped out half her population. The German merchants of the all-powerful Hanseatic League moved in solidly to gain control of the trade

2   *Vigeland – the main column, Frogner Park, Oslo*

3 The royal palace, Oslo,
and the statue of Queen
Maud

4 Statue of the late king,
Håkon VII, in Oslo

arteries that flowed through Bergen, a grip that was to last 200 years.

In 1397 the Danish Queen Margaret managed to bring about the triple union of Norway, Sweden, and Denmark. It was an uneasy union, and although Norway and Denmark remained united until 1814 there were frequent disputes and break-ups with Sweden, which finally dropped out in 1521. Through all her years of union Norway reaped no benefit at all, practically ignored – except when taxes were due or fighting men needed – by the Danish kings far away in Copenhagen. From the start Danes received all the plum posts of administration in Norway, and high-handed Danish action lost Norway her long-held sovereignty rights over the Hebrides and the Isle of Man. This was later to be followed by a similar loss of the Orkneys and the Shetland Islands. But the final degradation came when Norway lost her status as a separate kingdom through an illegal Danish action that proclaimed her to be part of Denmark, involving her at the same time in the Danish acceptance of the reformed Lutheran Church. Norwegian monasteries and convents were destroyed on Danish orders.

But having touched rock bottom Norway began to surface again, in spite of many setbacks on the way. By the end of the seventeenth century the swing into a new phase of prosperity was firmly assured. Christian IV was the first of the Danish kings to direct his conscience towards his northern realm, which he visited many times, studying her problems, and doing what he could to help. When Oslo was rebuilt after a fire he paid it the compliment of having it renamed Christiania after himself.

By the end of the eighteenth century, with the Great Nordic War behind her and blossoming with a rich peasant art, Norway was secure in a steadily increasing population and strengthened economy. There dawned in Christiania a new richness of culture and sophistication, much influenced by English modes and manners. This made the blow all the greater when Frederik VI committed Norway, although her sympathies were entirely pro-British, to an alliance with Napoleon. She was further drawn by

Denmark into a war against Sweden that was not of her choosing. Everything reached a climax when Frederik VI, crushed by Swedish forces, signed a peace treaty in which he handed Norway over to Sweden, in spite of having no right to dispose of an unconquered nation even though he was ruler of it. Norway refused to recognize the treaty.

For centuries Norway had been unable to elect her own leaders, but now everything changed. A National Assembly of 112 elected representatives met at Eidsvold, north of Christiania, to lay the foundation of a constitution. On 17 May 1814 the democratic constitution came into being, and this occasion is celebrated annually with as much enthusiasm and light-heartedness as if the ink were still wet on the paper.

So much could have gone against this brave action at Eidsvold. As it was there followed a period of cliff-hanging suspense while 45,000 well-armed Swedish troops clashed with 25,000 poorly armed Norwegians, but negotiations finally brought about a peaceful alliance with Sweden pledged to respect and uphold the new Norwegian constitution. The Storting (parliament) in Christiania graciously elected Carl XIII of Sweden king of Norway.

It is no coincidence that in the clean, fresh wind of freedom there was a tremendous upsurging in the worlds of art, music, literature and in other fields of achievement. Names like Henrik Ibsen, Edvard Grieg, Bjørnstjerne Bjørnson, Ole Bull, Edvard Munch, Roald Amundsen, Fridtjof Nansen, and countless others became known throughout the world, a flow of brilliant minds and talents that has continued by way of Sigrid Undset, Tarjei Vesaas, and Kirsten Flagstad, among many more, to Thor Heyerdahl of the present day.

The Storting set the affairs of the country to rights, but disagreements with Sweden arose over many matters from Norway's insistence on having her own flag to her demands for a separate consular service. In 1905 the two nations again trembled on the brink of war, but this time Norway was armed and prepared. Fortunately the final break came peaceably, and Norway invited

5 *Briksdalsbreen, an arm of the Jostedal glacier, near Olden*

Prince Carl of Denmark to become king, taking the vacant throne. He was 33 years old, married to Princess Maud of England, and had a two-year-old son.

Although willing to be king, Prince Carl wanted the people of Norway to express their opinion, and the result was a nation-wide ballot that went overwhelmingly in his favour. He chose to be known as Håkon vii, and with a gesture that endeared him immediately to the nation he stepped ashore at Christiania with his young son, Crown Prince Olav, in his arms. The King's first words were 'All for Norway!', which was the motto that he lived by for the rest of his days.

His reign saw many hard times. Norway remained neutral in World War I, but nearly 50 per cent of her mercantile shipping was sunk in the all-out war of the German submarines. Economic depression followed in the years afterwards. And in the 30s a retired army officer, who called his party 'National Unity', failed to get a single seat in the Storting. His name was Vidkun Quisling.

The dawn of 9 April 1940 saw the invasion of Norway by Germany. Without any declaration of war the German forces swept in on her. The King, the Crown Prince, and the government were forced to flee from Oslo. Quisling tried to set up some sort of government on his own, and gave the world a new name for traitor. British aid was sent to Norway, but the hard-fought campaign was short-lived, and the King, refusing to surrender, left Norway on 7 June 1940 with the Crown Prince and the government on the British cruiser *Devonshire* to take up his exile in London. He was followed to Britain by thousands of his countrymen, who joined the Free Norwegian Forces there. At sea every ship in Norway's large mercantile fleet escaped capture by the Germans, and thus helped to win the Battle of the Atlantic for the Allies. Exactly five years to the day that he had left, King Håkon returned to liberated Norway amid scenes of wild rejoicing. He died in 1957, having never lost his Danish accent, and was succeeded by his only son, Crown Prince Olav. The tomb of Håkon vii is in Akerhus fortress in the heart of Oslo.

King Olav v was born at Sandringham in England, and studied

at Balliol College, Oxford, but he is a true Norseman in his love of
the snow and sea. In his youth he opened the famous Holmenkollen ski-meeting by making the first jump, and as a yachts-
man he is internationally acclaimed. It is a familiar sight to see
him sailing in Oslo fjord, and among his many racing trophies
there is an Olympic gold medal.

His wife, the late Crown Princess Märtha, was of the Swedish
royal family, but all three of their children have married Norwegian commoners. Princess Ragnhild and Princess Astrid were
the first to marry morganatically, but there was no smooth sailing
when it came to Crown Prince Harald's choice of a bride: a true
Cinderella story hit the headlines.

Crown Prince Harald met Sonja Haraldsen in 1958. He was a
student at the Norwegian Military Academy at the time, and later
studied at Balliol as his father had done. She was the daughter of
an Oslo shop-owner. For ten years their love for each other withstood strong opposition from all sides. It was a strange paradox
that the Norwegian people, who had been so proud of his democratic upbringing, his attendance at a local primary school, his
mixing as an ordinary cadet and student, should have expected
him to marry automatically someone of royal blood. But the story
has a happy ending. King Olav himself finally used the king's
right under the constitution to approve the match. Crown Prince
Harald and Sonja Haraldsen were married in Oslo Cathedral on
29 August 1968.

Crown Princess Sonja, beautiful and talented, whose status as a
commoner had been the only barrier, has since won over the Norwegian people. The birth of a daughter, Martha Louise, to the
popular couple in September 1971 was an occasion for much
rejoicing.

King Olav has seen his country with its highly developed social
welfare system return to a prosperity far beyond anything ever
known before. Gone for ever are the days when the peasant
farmers turned to harvest the sea in winter to supplement the poor
returns that the land gave them. Today agriculture is highly
mechanized, although such is the Norwegians' love of horses that

many farms still have one, so that the beautiful, cream-coloured Westland 'fjord pony' is a familiar and picturesque sight. Forestry and fishing are of major importance today as they have always been, but Norway is now primarily an industrial nation, secure and flourishing, sending her highly sophisticated products out into world-wide markets. Another tremendous source of income is her merchant shipping fleet, which is the third largest in the world. A rather surprising export is Norway's pure spring water, naturally filtered through stone and exported in millions of gallons. Whaling, due to international agreement, is now almost negligible, but the sea, which has always been generous to Norway, is yielding up new treasure in the gas and oil present in her territorial waters.

All this enables the Norwegians, who have a higher life expectancy over the age of 40 than any other nation, to enjoy an extremely high standard of living that so far seems to have escaped the backlash that follows in the wake of affluence. Crimes of violence and sexual crimes are rare, and when bank-raids take place it is almost always a Swedish car making for the border that is hunted by the police. With so much space and a glimpse of mountain, fjord or open countryside from even the meanest window, it is no wonder that there is hardly any vandalism. Penalties for drinking and driving are immediate imprisonment and the automatic loss of the driving licence. Fines are also heavy for exceeding the speed limit, which is a maximum of 80 k.p.h. (50 m.p.h.) throughout the country (it is as well to remember that radar control checks all the main roads). At parties, or when taking a moderate amount of wine when out to dinner, one person will abstain from drinking in order to drive the others home, or else all will travel by taxi. This has nothing to do with alcoholism, which is an old problem that has resulted in some strangely archaic drinking laws, so that many people make their own 'fire-water' and aggravate the situation. The price of spirits and even beer, which comes as a shock to tourists used to the cheaper rates or more southern climes, is another reason why otherwise law-abiding citizens have a still hidden in their cellars.

The state-owned Vinmonopol stores have a monopoly on the

selling of spirits, which includes Norway's well-known Linje Aquavit, so called because it was discovered long ago that taking it across the Equator (Linje) mellowed the spirit, giving it a distinctive flavour. Today it still makes the journey by boat from Norway to Australia and back again.

Norway is a country hooked on sport and keeping fit. Norwegian youth has an almost fanatical desire to excel in all fields of sport, and particularly on skis. There is hardly a Norwegian male who has not longed at some time to jump at Holmenkollen, the annual ski-meeting that attracts a regular attendance of no less than 100,000 spectators, who gather to watch the best skiers from all parts of the world compete there. Cross-country ski-racing, jumping contests, slalom and downhill, as well as speed-skating, keep the whole nation on the move in winter, and the mountains and the sea absorb everybody in the summertime.

This national obsession with sport was summed up with a civilized sense of the absurd in a cartoon that appeared during a general election: on television a politician was promising higher wages, lower taxes, and bigger pensions, but his family audience, sunk in their armchairs, listened with bored disinterest until in a flash all became electrified by his final words. 'With our party in power I promise you that Norway will take first, second, and third places at the next Holmenkollen!'

There also predominates amongst the Norwegians a quiet, personal pride in work, home, and nation, which exists together with a strong sense of responsibility towards people of other lands less fortunate than themselves. This has shown itself in countless ways over the years; one example was Fridtjof Nansen's great work for the refugees after World War I when he was estimated to have saved the lives of 6,400,000 children and 400,000 adults. Even immediately after the savagery of the German Occupation in World War II the Norwegians opened their homes to give food and comfort – paying the fares out of their own pockets – to the hungry, war-shattered children of their former oppressors.

Without doubt this concern for others does stem from a deep-rooted knowledge of what it means to live with danger and hardship. Nature has shaped Norway violently, and there is inherent in the Norwegians an awareness of how deeply life is involved with nature. This affinity with earth and rock, sea and waterfall, sky and air, penetrates every aspect of their country's economic structure, its arts, its folklore, and even the Norwegian language, which the great poet, Bjørnstjerne Bjørnson, once compared to an eagle chained to a rock, unable to display its strength and beauty because so few outside Norway understood it, and so much was lost in translation.

A tremendous variety of dialects dramatizes the Norwegian language. A great pride is taken in retaining them, and it is still often possible to slot a man into a particular valley, town, or island, at the moment that he opens his mouth. It was while visiting the home of Bjørnstjerne Bjørnson at Aulestad, now preserved as a museum, that I witnessed a perfect example of this district identification when Inge (my Norwegian husband) and the guide promptly recognized and pin-pointed each other's dialects; thus they found that they had been on neighbouring islands in their youth.

The Norwegian language was included in the effort to sweep away all traces of the Danish domination after the constitution. In 1850 a new-old language, now known as 'Nynorsk' (New Norwegian) was introduced in an effort to return to pure Norwegian, but the old Danish–Norwegian, known as 'Riksmål', then 'Bokmål', continued. Although an amalgamation of Nynorsk and Bokmål has not been officially brought about it does seem that both languages, which share equal status, have settled down comfortably together, and a natural blending will be the eventual outcome of it all.

Norway's other language is English. It is taught at an early age in school, and many Norwegians cynically declare that it has become their first language, so many phrases having been drawn into everyday use and the national Press being particularly fond of sprinkling its pages with English words, all of great benefit to the tourist industry.

Everywhere in Norway there prevails a warm hospitality that

makes the tourist feel more like a guest than a customer – when the announcement came that British tourists were to be restricted to a £50 travel allowance, a Norwegian newspaper carried an appeal that everything possible should be done 'to help our visiting British friends'.

The first tourist ever to record his impressions of Norway was the Greek, Pytheas, who landed in 'Ultima Thule', as he called it, after sailing north-east from the Shetlands. He wrote with amazement of the sun shining in the night. Much later there were visitors who told of Norsemen who flew like birds with wooden wings on their feet, but it was the Victorians who discovered the salmon fishing, the mountain climbing, and the pleasures of holidays spent sailing up the fjords. The element of surprise is still there for the present-day tourist, who finds that he can have a whole mountain, or a bay for swimming, or even a road all to himself. No wonder Norway is often advertised as the country 'to unwind in'.

2. Oslo

'Now I know how an Oslo seagull feels!' It was a young Norwegian girl, her face framed by long, silky-fair hair under her scarlet student-cap, who expressed these words on the public gallery of the Observation Tower on Tryvann Hill. She had flung out her arms as though to embrace the whole of the city that lay far below in its setting of forest and hills, lakes, rivers, and farmland, its twin-towered town hall standing like a gateway at the head of the long fjord that stretches away over 66 miles out to sea, busy with boats, hazy with seagulls. Forming a background were the distant peaks of the Norefjell range, Mount Gausta, Jonsnuten, and many others, rising against the enamel-blue sky.

But the seagull student did not spend long admiring the view. Perhaps going to the top of the tower had been just one more light-hearted excursion on that day in late spring, which is the time of celebrating the forthcoming end of their secondary schooling by the *Russ*. These young people spot the city with scarlet in their peaked baker-boy caps, the knots in the tasselled cords of each showing how many nights have been spent swotting until dawn; all are decked out in scarlet waistcoats decorated with the emblems of their individual schools, the boys carry walking sticks trimmed with scarlet ribbons, and the girls umbrellas in the same brave colour that is picked up by the Norwegian flag that flutters on all sides. Those matriculating with the final *examen artium*, which qualifies them for entrance to either university or college, are entitled to wear the more elaborate black cap with the heavy corded tassel, which rests by tradition on the right shoulder, on all occasions of importance throughout their lives.

These caps, both scarlet and black, are very much in evidence every 17 May when Norway celebrates Constitution Day, not with a display by the armed forces, but with processions of children, who afterwards take part in sports events and various festivities arranged specially for them all over the country. This delightful custom originated at Aulestad in the nineteenth century when the great author and poet, Bjørnstjerne Bjørnson, used to give cakes and fruit to the village children who came to visit him and bring him flowers on Norway's national day.

All over Norway people enjoy the public holiday, but nowhere is the celebrating more colourful than in Oslo. Through the crowd-lined streets hundreds and hundreds of school children and students, led by equally youthful brass bands, parade in a gloriously seething mass, all waving flags. In their schooldays the royal princesses were always among the throng. It takes over an hour for the procession to pass the royal palace where King Olav, following a tradition laid down by his father, waves to the children from the balcony in what must be the most informal march-past in the world.

Constitution Day is a good day for seeing how merry the Norwegians can be, for they are often unjustly accused of being too solid and serious by those who do not know them. But any day is a good day in Oslo with its easy informality, its excellent food, its climate of dry summer heat and crisp winter cold, its friendliness, and the air that is scented by forest, flowers, and sea. Within a short radius of the city's centre it is possible to sail between islands, swim from a bathing beach, or walk in the silent forests of the Oslomarka. Its colour appeals to the eye – the bright sun-umbrellas of the open-air cafés, the blossoming window-boxes that soften the starkness of tall flats, the pristine whiteness of the Monolith in Frogner Park, and even the warm red-brown of the town hall, which has been likened so often by the Norwegians themselves to a vast slab of goat cheese.

On the west wall of the town hall there is a sculptured relief of

Harald Hardråde, who founded Oslo about 1048 when he needed a strategic military site. There he sits on horseback, crown on head, Viking sword in hand, caught in a moment of glory when the last Viking raid on England, and the battle of Stamford Bridge with its fatal outcome, were still far from him. The ruins of the palace and the Maria Church that he built are to be seen in the park at Sørenga.

Yet King Harald Hardråde does not figure in Oslo's coat-of-arms, which instead depicts St Hallvard, the city's patron saint, holding three arrows and a millstone, seated on a lion-headed stool with a woman that he had gallantly attempted to rescue lying at his feet. He was a young nobleman, related to the king, and was about to row across the fjord one day when a woman came rushing up to him, and implored him to save her from being killed for a theft that she had not committed. He pulled her on board, and rowed off in the direction of his father's house, using all his powerful strength to send the boat shooting across the water, but the men giving chase followed in another boat, and soon came alongside. When Hallvard refused to surrender the woman, of whose innocence he was convinced, one of the men shot and killed him with an arrow, and then their quarry was brutally murdered. But Hallvard's body, in spite of being tied to a mill-stone, floated to the surface, and in view of such a miraculous happening he was proclaimed a saint. The whole story is illustrated in sculptured relief above the main entrance to the town hall.

Near by in the Minnepark, Gamlebyen (the old town), archaeologists have excavated the foundations of St Hallvard's Church, which was the ecclesiastical centre of medieval Oslo. It was this church, dedicated to Oslo's patron saint, that saw the coronation in 1299 of Håkon V, who made Oslo the capital.

Close at hand is Ladegården, the bishop's palace, once the most fortified stronghold in the city, the remains of which form the foundations of part of the present building. It was to the bishop's palace that Mary Stuart's son, James VI, soon to be James I of England, came with full sail across the North Sea to wed his Danish bride Anne, who had been landed at Oslo when the ship carrying her from Copenhagen to Scotland had been blown off course. James blamed the storm on witchcraft, and one of history's most notorious witch trials (during it one witch professed to know what the royal couple had said to each other on their wedding night in Ladegården) took place in Scotland afterwards.

Apart from the fortress of Akerhus, which dates from 1300 and occupies such a commanding position on a rock overlooking the harbour and fjord, very little else remains of the old city that was destroyed by fire in 1624. King Christian iv came from Copenhagen to supervise personally the planning of the new town, and it was he who decided that the streets should be the width that they are today – almost 50 feet – and that the buildings were to be of stone. It was then that the capital became Christiania, changing slightly to Kristiania in the 1870s with the abolition of the Danish 'C', but on 1 January 1925 the old Viking name of Oslo was restored to it.

It is an easy city to explore when armed with a street map. To aid the visiting motorist there is the Tourist Pilot Service, which consists of squads of authorized youths and girls on motor scooters, neatly uniformed and crash-helmeted, who are to be found on the quayside when landing, outside Vigeland Park, and other prominent sites, ready to lead the way *free of charge* to any sight or destination that has been selected within the city limits. Other towns, such as Bergen and Tønsberg, offer this service, which is financed by an oil company. On a bus nobody need fear alighting at the wrong spot: I once saw three young Frenchmen, unable to speak a word of either English or Norwegian, get off too soon on their way to Oslo's Postal Museum. The bus had already started up when the conductor missed them. Immediately he stopped the bus, and ran back down the road after them! He returned in triumph, his three rather bewildered Frenchmen in tow, and a mile farther on he allowed them to alight, indicating with a wave the direction that they were to follow.

The town hall is an excellent point from which to start seeing the city, and a pleasant few minutes can be spent looking across Rådhusplassen with its fountains and groups of bronze figures to the ships and small craft in the harbour that are for ever coming and going. Down by the water people are buying freshly caught and cooked prawns from the fishing-boats tied up at the piers. From this spot organized fishing trips on the Oslo fjord leave with tackle provided free, as well as motor launches with guides aboard that take the most beautiful trips through the islands and skerries. Although the public transport steamers are merely going about their business they provide an inexpensive way of sailing across the harbour area past the Dyna lighthouse to explore the wooded suburb of Nesoddtangen. The hydrofoil also departs from the harbour to touch at various places down the fjord.

Facing Rådhusplass on the east side is a statue of Franklin D. Roosevelt, who in a famous wartime speech held Norway up as an example to the free world. In 1940 he sent a warship specially to neutral Sweden to fetch away to the safety of the United States Crown Princess Märtha and the three royal children, who had been rushed to refuge there at the time of the German invasion. Winston Churchill visited Oslo after the liberation and stood on the steps of the town hall with tears running down his face, acknowledging the tremendous cheers of the city.

Along the steps are bronze statues by Per Palle Storm of the workmen who built the town hall. The foundation stone was laid in 1931, but the building was not formally opened until 1950, and then as part of the celebrations held to commemorate Oslo's 900th anniversary. Its rather sombre outer appearance does not prepare the first-time visitor for the dazzling interior that has been almost excessively decorated by many of Norway's leading painters and sculptors of that intervening period. It boasts the largest painting in Europe, a mural entitled 'The People at Work and Play', painted in oils on wooden plates by Henrik Sørensen, a leading figure in Norwegian art.

It takes little time to cross Rådhusplassen and find a ferry at the pier to take the seven-minute trip across to the peninsula of Bygdøy, where you can see three of the most interesting old ships in the world, and certainly the most famous of all rafts – the *Kon Tiki*. The Viking ships with their superb lines rise black against the white walls and domed roofs of the individual wings of the hall that houses them. Known as the Oseberg ship, the Gokstad ship, and the Tune ship, all had been drawn up on to the shores of Oslo fjord to be used as burial ships, and after the dead had been laid in them, together with all that was needed for the journey to the next world, earth and rocks and stones were used to bury them.

The Oseberg ship was the richest find of all, and was excavated in 1904, not far from Tønsberg, which was the district occupied by the Ynglinge dynasty, who claimed descent from the god Odin himself. They were a powerful line of kings whose blood ran through the veins of Harald Fairhair. The ship, built of oak in the ninth century, is 68 feet long, over 16 feet wide at its broadest part, its stakes are fixed to the ribs with lashings of whale bristle, and it was constructed as all Viking ships were to be wonderfully sea-worthy and elastic. The tall prow, richly carved with strange, fantastic animals all intertwined, terminates most gracefully in a spiral tipped by a serpent's head, and the stern, which is similar, ends in the curling flick of the serpent's tail. It would have been rowed by 30 men when not under sail, and 15 pairs of oars were found among the grave-goods. The rudder, which could easily be swung up in shallow water, lies like a great oar on the starboard side aft. Perhaps Queen Åse, whose burial ship it almost certainly was, often travelled in it, for it was low-built for coastal sailing, and not for plundering raids across the sea.

Queen Åse was the grandmother of Harald Fairhair, who united Norway, and in a specially built burial chamber on the ship her old bones lay beside those of a young serving woman, who had been put to death in order to attend her royal mistress in after life. Everything the Queen might need for her comfort was there too, from quilts and pillows and tapestries to small domestic items, such as iron scissors, a comb, a yarn-winder, lamps, and even spare pairs of shoes designed to fit her swollen arthritic feet. Fifteen horses were slaughtered and placed in the ship, together with an ox, and four dogs; tethering ropes and pegs and dog-chains being added thoughtfully along with them. Three ornate sleighs, a beautiful cart with scenes from the sagas carved into its oaken planks, and a working sled, together with kitchen utensils, weaving looms, studded chests, and jewellery boxes were among many other objects that came to light. Present-day Norwegian needlewomen take great pride in being able to execute the Oseberg stitch, which was used in the intricate embroidery on linen found among the Queen's effects. Most of the treasures uncovered, both rich and humble, are on display in the fourth wing of the hall, and include objects from the Gokstad ship, all of which combine to give a splendid insight into the daily life of a Viking household.

The Gokstad and the Tune ships were both built for heavy seas, for use in raids and for trading. The sagas tell of the exceptional handsomeness and great height, the courage and daring of the 50-year-old Viking King Olav Geirstad-Alv, Queen Åse's stepson, whose bones were found in the Gokstad ship. It would have had a crew of 32 oarsmen, and the remains of 64 shields, which had hung like a row of overlapping scales along the sides of the ship, were uncovered with a variety of grave-goods, as well as the bones of 12 horses and 6 dogs. The most surprising find was the skeleton and feathers of a peacock, which must have been a rare prize that Olav Geirstad-Alv had brought home in triumph from some eastern shore.

Not far from the Viking Ship Hall, down a hill that gives a fine view of the harbour between the trees, there are a couple of wedge-shaped buildings that are constructed on the lines of traditional boat-houses. In one is the Maritime Museum, and in the other is the *Fram*, the tough little Polar exploration ship that was built for Fridtjof Nansen's 1893–6 expedition by a well-known Norwegian marine architect of the day, Colin Archer, who was of British descent.

In the *Fram* Nansen expected to drift in the Polar ice to the North Pole, but after two years of drifting, and the Pole still far away, he and a single companion left the ship, taking dogs, sledges and kayaks. They reached the highest latitude then attained, but were forced to spend the winter of 1895–6 in the area now known as Fridtjof Nansen Land, suffering terrible hardships.

An expedition sent from England, led by Frederick Jackson, met Nansen and his companion who returned with it, the *Fram* sailing home soon afterwards.

Children and adults alike find the *Fram* fascinating, for apart from its aura of adventurous voyages, you are allowed to go on board and below decks. The steamer is pointed fore and aft, has three masts, an engine of 220 h.p. and is fat as a tub in shape, which, together with the special strength of her construction enabled her to penetrate the ice without being crushed. In the cabins are displayed stores, equipment, clothes, maps and furs, not only from Nansen's expedition, but from when Otto Sverdrup explored vast areas north of the American continent in her, and also from the time when Roald Amundsen used her to beat Captain Scott to the South Pole.

The next step at Bygdøy is to a more exotic-looking building than those already visited. This houses the *Kon Tiki*, the balsa-wood raft on which in 1947 Thor Heyerdahl drifted for 101 days with his five companions across the Pacific Ocean from Peru to the Polynesian island of Raroia. The *Kon Tiki* is splendidly displayed as though in full sail at sea. The golden-coloured raft with its sun-god on the sail was constructed in the same way as those made in Peru in A.D. 500, and on her Heyerdahl proved his long-held belief that prehistoric South Americans could have sailed on balsawood rafts across the sea to people the islands of Polynesia. His log books are there in glass cases, and it is fascinating to read in his own hand of those final dramatic moments before *Kon Tiki* broke up on the coral reef. In another hall beneath the first it is as though you are in the depths of the sea underneath the raft, which appears to be floating overhead. The fearsome whale shark is shooting by, and also suspended there are the other sea creatures that were written about in Heyerdahl's account of that exciting voyage.

Also at Bygdøy is the open air Folk Museum. In one of the main buildings is Ibsen's study, containing his desk, chair, and writing materials. Outside in the acres of parkland, set amid trees and lakes, are 150 wooden houses, barns and workshops, dating from the Middle Ages, that have been gathered from all over Norway, each section representing a particular district. All are fully furn-ished and equipped, giving a complete and very vivid picture of how life has been lived throughout the centuries; everything is there from the picturesque old sleighs used for transport to the great drinking bowls, wooden and gaily painted, which were filled with strong liquor and passed around to all the company in turn on festive occasions. On some of the tables are the carved butter moulds, which presented the butter in beautiful shapes, intricately patterned, on special raised stands; butter is still served in these lovely traditional forms in many hotels and private homes.

The collection of buildings includes a very fine twelfth-century Stave church from Gol in Hallingdal, standing by the trees in its black-timbered, many-roofed magnificence. Only 25 of these unique stave churches are still in existence, and very few of them have been left in their original state. They get their name from the staves or poles that were used in their construction, and all were built within a framework of heavy pine timbers with turrets and spires ornamented by fang-tongued dragons which have the same aggressive beauty as the old Viking ships. Around the outer walls an ambulatory was added, and in one section there was always a small aperture through which lepers could hear the services being conducted inside.

Displays of folk dancing in national costume, often by children, give life and gaiety to this outdoor museum, and in each section the guides wear the traditional costume of their particular region. The style, design, and colour of these costumes vary distinctively from county to county, and there are even variations within the area: it would have been possible in the old days to tell by the pattern of the embroidery on a woman's bodice or skirt-hem whether she came from north or south of a certain valley. It must have been a great help in the past at occasions such as a 300-strong wedding party to be able to pick out at a glance those from the part of the country from which you wanted to hear the latest news or gossip.

Norwegian women of all ages take a great pride in wearing national costume, hand-woven, home-dyed and embroidered with wools in the traditional shades. The garments are extremely attractive and feminine, and can be worn for all occasions from school graduation to the wedding of a king. A guest can pay her hostess no greater compliment than arriving in costume, and vice versa. Naturally these outfits are costly, due to all the handwork involved, and they are worn with elaborate gold or silver brooches, often with a great deal of other expensive ornamentation as well. With such a costume in her wardrobe there is one great disadvantage for the Norwegian woman: she can never protest that she 'hasn't a thing to wear!'

The main street in Oslo is Karl Johan Gate, named after the Swedish king, Carl XIV, who became king of Norway in 1818 during the union with Sweden. Carl Johan had been Napoleon's General Jean Bernadotte, but was adopted into the Swedish royal family as heir and then monarch of Sweden. An equestrian statue of him stands in the forecourt of the royal palace on a rise at the head of Karl Johan Gate, although he never set foot in the residence that was built for him, dying before it was completed in 1848. It has been the official royal residence ever since, and there are no walls or gates to keep any distance between the king and his people. There is nothing to stop everybody enjoying the park that surrounds the palace, and in winter it is full of small children on skis. Two sentries of the royal guard are on duty by the double-doored entrance, their uniforms dark blue, their bowler-shaped hats trimmed with a magnificent burst of plumage. The changing of the guard always brings a little crowd of sightseers, who gather freely in the forecourt.

Steps in the palace park lead the way down into Karl Johan Gate, and soon you come to the University of Oslo on your left. It was established in 1811, and has since expanded far and wide in the Blindern area to the north of the city. But it is here in the forecourt that by tradition the new students gather on their first day at university, all in their black-tasselled caps, many of the girls in national custume, to be addressed from the steps of the Doric entrance by the chancellor.

In the Festival Hall, or Aula, of the university are the famous murals by Edvard Munch which were unveiled in 1916, bringing

7   *Oslo, the harbour and city hall*
8   *One of the three Viking ships preserved in Oslo*

9   *Nansen's polar exploration ship – the* Fram

to him at home the honour and recognition that he had already gained abroad. Above the rostrum, dominating the Aula, blazes 'The Sun', the fount of light and life, searing the eye with its brilliance as it radiates its vivid colours over fjord and cliff, setting the theme that passes through all the other murals, linking them into a magnificent whole that radiates an aura of its own. To the left of the rostrum is 'History', where an old man is seated under the branches of a great tree, its roots strong and lively in the rich earth, as he tells tales of days gone by to the young boy listening to him. On the opposite wall is 'Alma Mater' with the mother as the central figure, a baby at her breast, a child with a bunch of flowers at her side, while two more children are seated side by side near a tree. These three main murals, together with the others that are no less dramatic, symbolize the past and the future, wisdom and the quest for learning, life, death and birth again in the eternal cycle.

Around the corner from the university, located in Frediks Gate, is the Historisk Museum, which houses the University Collection of Antiquities that includes the not-to-be-missed 'Treasure Chamber', with exquisite gold and silver ornaments and jewellery from the Viking Age, all too frequently left out by the tourist in a hurry. This dazzling and priceless display, skilfully lighted to show each piece to advantage, with magnifying glasses arranged to allow full appreciation of the intricate work, will fill in any gaps left in an overall picture of Viking culture set out by the Viking ship exhibition at Bygdøy.

Here are the great rings, so often mentioned in the sagas, that were given as gifts by Viking kings, together with scabbards, spurs, and bridles for their horses all in pure gold, often ornamented with designs showing Odin, the god of war, and Tor with his mighty hammer.

Amid the necklets and armbands, the brooches, pendants, capepins and amulets – one finely fashioned necklace alone is made of two and a half pounds of pure gold – there are the exquisite adornments found at Vik in Sogn, which belonged to a woman of high birth, probably a queen. It was an age of gold, and the heaps of pay-gold bear witness to the way the Vikings would casually break any gold ornament on their person, however elaborate, for use as immediate payment. The gold coins that were brought back from foreign lands were not used at face value, but frequently worn as charms to keep away evil spirits and were broken up in turn as pay-gold when needed.

In one display case containing valuable trinkets that belonged to a Viking woman there is a large key, for the keys were always entrusted to the care of the womenfolk, who no doubt in the absence of their menfolk at war buried in the ground for safe-keeping much of the treasure on display, for none of it has been recovered from graves.

Back in the main thoroughfare again, the next few yards are those that were walked daily in his old age by the frock-coated, top-hatted figure of Henrik Ibsen, who went into the Grand Hotel every day for an apéritif, and by whom people could set their watches, so regular and so familiar was his appearance in Karl Johan Gate. Studenterlunden, the Students Park, lies between this street and Stortings Gate. It is leafy with trees, the fountains play, and sun-umbrellas give shade in the open-air cafés. Statues of Ibsen and Bjørnstjerne Bjørnson flank the entrance to the National Theatre.

The Storting (Parliament) is also in Studenterlunden, comprising an Upper House (Lagting) and a Lower House (Odelting); there are 150 members and the electoral period is four years. On 1 October there is a ceremonial opening of the Storting by King Olav in the presence of the Corps Diplomatique, and he is escorted from the palace and back again by a military procession. Guided tours of the building, which dates from 1861, are allowed at certain times.

Continuing on down Karl Johan Gate you come to Stortorvet (large market), the square in front of the cathedral, where market stalls blossom with flowers and every kind of potted plant, fruit, and vegetable is on sale.

Oslo Cathedral, which in 1971 saw the 900th anniversary of the Oslo diocese, has a copper roof and was built at the end of the seventeenth century, but has twice been restored. The ornately carved pulpit, rich in gilt and colour, and the triptych both date from 1699, but *al tempera* decorations on the vaulted ceiling, showing a beardless Christ, are from 1936–50 by Hugo Lous Mohr. The royal pew is a small private gallery. In August 1968, 2,500 roses and a profusion of other blooms were used to decorate the cathedral when Crown Prince Harald married Sonja Haraldsen. After the ceremony all the flowers were made up into hundreds of small bunches and delivered to the sick and elderly in Oslo.

Outside in a semi-circle round the cathedral are the Basarhalls, arcades that were once the centre of the city's food trade but are now an applied art centre – another harmonious blending of the old and new which seems to characterize Oslo. There is plenty to buy in this city and the high standards of its merchandise are encouraged by the Norwegian Design Centre, where exhibitions are held of products of outstanding design. The cheap and the tawdry have no market in Norway, for the Norwegians seem to have a built-in good taste, and look for elegance and quality when they buy.

There are many who might jokingly dispute this point of good taste after seeing the city's Frogner Park. It spreads out over 80 acres, and displays the monumental results of years of work in stone, iron, and bronze by the sculptor, Gustav Vigeland, who in 1921 made an agreement that in exchange for a studio built specially for him the city of Oslo should be entitled to all the works of art that he produced from that time forward. His talent is not in dispute, but in a way Oslo got more than it bargained for; the 150 sculptural groups together make an overpowering hymn to life in all its phases.

I first saw the park in winter. The bronze figures on the bridge were dark against the unmarked snow and white sky. They had downy caps of snow on their heads. I wandered along, looking at each in turn, all representing stages in human life from the small boy stamping in uncontrolled rage to the people trapped in the wheels of fate, unable to break loose. I thought wryly that it must be the bitter chill of the day that kept me detached from their loving and hating, their anger, frustration, and suffering, but I have since seen them at all seasons of the year, and the temperature had nothing to do with it. I had reacted towards them as everybody does. They depict the whole range of human emotion, but cannot touch the heart.

There are many steps to climb up to the base of the Monolith, which dominates the park, a shining white granite centrepiece from which 36 sculptural groups radiate. There are 121 figures making up the 55-feet-tall Monolith, and they struggle and clamber over each other, becoming children at the top. It has been called 'Man's Struggle for Light and Knowledge', but Gustav Vigeland himself said enigmatically that the Monolith was his religion, which leaves the interpretation of what is there to every individual who views it.

The park is a good spot to relax in with its open-air restaurant, sports arena, tennis courts, and a paddle boat that does trips on the lake. It is a place to take children, who love to stroke the smooth white stone heads of the sculptured babies that bawl and tumble and smile toothlessly. There is also the children's circle where eight bronze figures express the exuberance of childhood, and in the centre of it is the human embryo, the beginning of life itself. On hot days the toddlers and small children paddle and bathe unofficially in the water overflowing from the great fountain that gushes up with tremendous force from the vast basin held by six nude giants; older children and adults go to the open-air swimming-pool to which international swimming contests attract large crowds.

The rose garden in the park is of particular interest to British visitors as it has links with the days of World War II when King Håkon resided in London. On that first Christmas of 1940 right through to the last one of his exile in 1945 Norwegian commandos, returning to Norway on secret missions, dug up a fir tree and took it back to London for the King's Christmas. When the war was over the people of Oslo decided that the custom should continue, but now they would send the tallest and best tree in their forests to stand annually at Christmas in Trafalgar Square, proclaiming their thanks for all that was done for their king in those hard years. In 1953 the people of London sent a rose garden to the people of Oslo in appreciation of the annual Christmas tree, and it was planted in Vigeland Park.

To help you understand what it was like in Norway during that time of Occupation there is a Resistance Museum in the fortress of Akerhus. Photographs and newspapers, relics and models show everything from the impact of that fateful day of the German attack in April 1940, right through to the liberation. 'It is a clear record of the facts, and quite without hatred. I am pleased and thankful that it has been done that way,' said one Norwegian, who had suffered during the Occupation. Near by in the grounds there is a simple monument to the Norwegian patriots who were executed by German firing squads against a high bank, which is now a memorial garden.

On the opposite side of the fjord, about seven miles south-west of Oslo is the Sonja Henie–Niels Onstad Art Centre at Høvikodden. This collection of twentieth-century art, much of it from the postwar period, was donated by the skating champion and filmstar, Sonja Henie, and her husband, leading shipowner and art collector, Niels Onstad. Together with funds for the construction and maintenance of the free, sculpturally-designed building, it was the largest private donation ever made in Norway, totalling over 50,000,000 kroner.

The Centre was designed by two young Norwegian architects, Jon Eikvar and Evein-Erik Engebretsen, and the five blocks containing the exhibition halls project above the roof surface of the other parts of the building, and the terraces have a panoramic view of the fjord, the whole surrounded by park and woodland. Apart from special exhibitions there is a permanent collection of 250 paintings, including work by Picasso, Matisse, Juan Gris, Bazaine, Manessier, Riopelle, and many others, as well as the younger expressionists such as Jorn, Appel, Corneille, and Alechinsky. The concert hall of the Centre, hung with dramatic paintings by Pierre Soulages, its décor brown and white, is another asset of the city of Oslo, and there are also an open-air theatre, a restaurant and a cafeteria.

The Onstads' home being not far away on an island in the Oslo fjord, Sonja Henie was present almost all the time when the Centre was being built, watching a dream come true. The Centre was opened in 1968, and a year later she died on her way home by plane from France. A special room holds the skating trophies and medals that she won during her lifetime: the medals of ten world championships and three Olympic golds take pride of place in the trophy room, and among all those many elaborate trophies is a small silver-handled paper knife – the first prize she ever won.

The National Gallery in Oslo is important for its collection of Norwegian art. Here are the landscapes of Johan C. Dahl (1788–1857) who was the first painter of note to portray the magnificence of Norway's scenery, and Mathias Stoltenberg's fresh and lively portraits of country folk, to mention just two of the artists represented. Christian Krogh's very large and famous painting 'The Discovery of America' hangs on the south staircase, and shows the Viking Leif Eiriksson sighting America 500 years before Columbus set sail. This must have been reproduced in Norway almost as many times as 'The Laughing Cavalier' in England!

There is a section devoted to Edvard Munch, the only Norwegian painter to influence decisively art trends beyond his own country, a pioneer of expressionism in Germany and Scandinavia. Some of his most famous paintings, including 'Girls on the Bridge' and 'The Sick Child' are housed here, but the majority of his paintings are in the magnificent Munch Museum, which was opened in 1963. He was born in 1863 in Hedmark, and the following year his parents moved to Oslo. He was only five years old when his mother died, followed nine years later by his sister, Sophie. The theme of grief recurs constantly in his paintings, together with the agony of jealousy. He once quarrelled violently with Gustav Vigeland when they shared a mistress, and the feud lasted for the rest of their lives. He was neurotic, and suffered from bouts of ill health, but he was a kind-hearted, sensitive, and likeable man, said to be the most handsome in all Scandinavia. When he died in 1944 he bequeathed to the city of Oslo all his works that were still in his possession; they numbered hundreds, for from 1909 he had refused to part with anything, wanting to have his work all around him, even hanging them in the fruit trees in his garden to weather the colours to his liking.

In this museum can be seen the famous painting 'The Cry'. Munch said of it that it depicted a moment when he stood looking out over the fjord when the sun was setting, leaving the sky blood-red, and it seemed to him that the whole of nature screamed. 'The Cry' was part of his 'Frieze of Life' that was never completed, but all his life he dreamed of decorating a room with a series of pictures that would collectively present the cycle of life. Although it never came about he was spurred on by this ambition to heights of achievement that caused him to produce so many masterpieces, and to take his place as one of the world's great painters and print-makers.

There are several artists' centres in Oslo where it is possible to buy contemporary Norwegian art. Near the town hall there is the Artists' Association centre where there are exhibitions, and the Young Artists' Society in the same area holds changing exhibitions of ceramics, prints and paintings where there might be a chance to spot another Munch.

The famous Baldishol tapestry, which is considered to be the finest and oldest woven tapestry in Europe, comparable only to the embroidered Bayeux tapestry, is to be seen in the Museum of Fine Arts. It depicts Norsemen of the Middle Ages in all seasons of the year, and although no longer complete it shows that even then there was that sense of personal harmony with nature that characterizes the Norwegian today. Of particular delight are the full-breasted birds in the April woods that perch rather stiffly on branches around the figure of a walker, their colours blue, black, green and ochre against a rust-red background, and in the section showing the month of May a brave knight on horseback rides through a blue field thick with flowers.

Husfliden (the Norwegian Association for Home Arts and Crafts) is a non-profit organization marketing the work of country craftsmen, and these shops, with their hand-woven, hand-carved and home-knitted goods of exceptional quality, are to be found in Oslo and other towns throughout Norway. They give the tourist the chance to buy 'the real thing', and ensure that there is no danger of the old arts and crafts of the valleys dying out.

Everywhere the *Gullsmed* (Goldsmiths) sell almost exclusively Norwegian work of gold, silver and hand-beaten pewter. Their slogan is 'A Gift from a Goldsmith is a Gift for Life', and even the smallest purchase is automatically attractively gift-wrapped. In all shops, if mention is made that the purchase is a gift, an attractive bow and patterned paper will be used at no extra charge. Above all, a friendly and helpful attitude exists in shops, as well as in all other places where the public is served.

Naturally enough in a country devoted to the open air the Oslo sports shops offer everything from fishing permits for angling in Oslomarka to clubs for the Bogstad golf course. After looking at gleaming racks of skis it is interesting to compare them with the equally elegantly shaped 2,500-year-old Øvrebo ski-tip in the Ski Museum, which is housed in the building under the Holmenkollen ski-jump itself and contains the oldest collection of skiing gear in the world. It shows the development of skis, bindings and poles, and includes a ski-maker's workshop.

The Holmenkollen ski-jump stands silhouetted high against the sky over Lake Besserud, and is flanked by the tiered stands. There is a lift to the high tower, which in winter takes the jumpers up the 183 feet to the top. Quite apart from the magnificent view you get an excellent impression of what it is like to face one of the most testing jumps in the world. In summer a wrought-iron figure of a skier in full flight hangs suspended at the point where the leap into space begins, but winter seems far away to those bathing in Lake Besserud far below, or using the stands for a rest in the sun.

To be at Holmenkollen or the nearby Frogner Saeter on a soft summer evening is to see the pale, translucent Nordic dusk settle over Oslo and the fjord beyond. Then it becomes a city of light which spreads out into the ships and boats on the water that shimmers in the distance as far as the eye can see.

3. Bergen

It does rain in Bergen. Nobody would deny that, least of all the Bergensers, who boast of their unpredictable weather, and feel that an umbrella should be incorporated into the town's-coat-of-arms. Everybody carries one, even when the sun shines. Yet it is amazing how many times you can visit Bergen without getting a drop of rain.

To approach Bergen by water is to see it suddenly appear as the rocky, wooded sides of the fjord slide back like curtains, and there it lies, spread out from a thick, clustering nucleus of pastel-coloured buildings with roofs of russet, grey, and copper-green to reach far up the pine-clad slopes of seven mountains.

'I greet you, Princess of the Seas, King Olav Kyrre's ancient city . . .' These are the words from one of the songs without number that have been sung in praise of Bergen since days lost in time when the boats came down from the North with cargoes of dried fish to trade. Bergen's prosperity has been founded on fish and trade, and today with its university and colleges it is the second largest city in Norway, a busy centre of commerce, and the cultural heart of the west coast. It is a cosmopolitan city, long used to the coming and going of foreign merchants and their ships, and the arts have flourished in its rich atmosphere.

The hub of Bergen is its harbour. The green water, creamy with the wakes of big ships, trawlers and ferries, lies embraced by the arms of the city with its broad avenues and ancient, narrow streets, its buildings old and new, its parks and wharves, its monuments to men of the sea, and statues of its famous sons. The composer,

Edvard Grieg, stands in the central park by the bandstand, Ole Bull with his fiddle is placed near Bergen's theatre, and dramatist Ludvig Holberg, the Molière of the North, looks imperiously over the bright awnings of the fish market and out to sea.

The Bergen fish market is famous. It has been there for centuries, backed by a bobbing forest of masts in the harbour. There the housewives come with their baskets to choose from the harvest of the sea being slapped about in a slithering display. Those who must have fish even fresher than the morning's catch will select what they want from tanks of live fish, and their choice is whisked up in a net, flopped down on a board, and promptly decapitated with a single blow of a heavy knife.

The fishermen, clumping about in their high boots on the wet cobbles, are as used to the tourists' cameras as they are to the sea, but occasionally they grin, eyes twinkling, and make a friendly remark to those taking photographs or recording their movements on film, for the people of Bergen are by nature warm-hearted and jovial, renowned for their sense of humour, their lilting dialect, and their pride in being Bergensers, which is almost clannish. It is an old joke to say: 'I'm not from Norway – I'm from Bergen'.

There were settlements on Bergen's site long before the city was founded in 1070 by the son of Harald Hardråde, King Olav Kyrre, who enjoyed music and the good things of life as the Bergensers do today. The chonicler, Snorre, wrote of Olav Kyrre in the sagas: 'He was a man of peace, and a most popular king, and during his reign Norway rose in riches and splendour'.

St Mary's Church on the north side of the harbour is associated with Snorre, who attended mass there before leaving Norway for the last time to return home to Iceland, which had been colonized by Norwegian Vikings in the ninth century. Appropriately his statue stands, the sagas under one arm, in front of St Mary's, which with its twin towers topped by pointed copper spires is the oldest building in Bergen, as well as being one of the loveliest romanesque churches in Norway. Its colourful baroque pulpit is truly magnificent, blazing like a great jewel in its ancient setting.

Another church to be viewed while in Bergen is the pitch-timbered Fantoft Stave Church with its pyramid roofs. It was built in Sogn in the twelfth century, and was moved to its present woodland site in 1883. The darkness of the interior of any stave church never fails to arouse comment, but both the Devil and the bitter cold had to be kept out in that age of glassless windows, and all apertures were kept as small as possible. Set in the outside wall of Fantoft Stave Church is a sacred touchstone, and present day tourists are no less eager to touch it than the awed and reverent pilgrims of the past.

Bergenhus Fortress, once a royal residence, stands at the approach to the harbour. Its ceremonial hall, known as Håkons Hall, is named after King Håkon Håkonssøn, for whom it was built between 1247 and 1261, and it was the setting for a great banquet when the king made his son, Magnus (the Law-Mender) joint monarch with himself, a happy arrangement that lasted until the old king died in the Orkneys. Magnus's granddaughter was the tragic little princess, known as the Maid of Norway, who died on board ship on her way to be Queen of Scotland. The Rosenkrantz Tower in the fortress, built later (1562–1567), also has Scottish links, for it was here that the Earl of Bothwell, husband of Mary, Queen of Scots, was held prisoner after his flight from Scotland. Both the Tower and Håkons Hall were damaged by an explosion in World War II, but they have been restored and the hall is used again for banquets and important occasions as it was in the past.

Not far from the fortress and on the quayside is Bryggen, a unique and picturesque collection of gabled wooden houses, their colours a mellow rust, ochre, grey and white, and they date back to medieval times when they were the property of the Hanseatic League. It was an ancient trading site long before the Norwegian kings sold out the trade monopoly to the German merchants, whose presence forced the Bergen traders to move to the other side of the harbour, making them surrender the right to worship in St Mary's Church, which became the Germans' parish church, the whole area being enclosed behind high timber walls. Today many painters, weavers, and craftsmen have their studios and workshops in Bryggen, some of which can be visited.

The Hanseatic museum is one of the best preserved and oldest of the wooden buildings, and it is possible to step back into the past and follow step by step, almost hour by hour, a day in the life of a Hanseatic merchant, his assistant and secretaries, and the eight apprentices submitted into his charge. No women were allowed in the area, all the merchants having to remain single during their time there, with only men doing the cooking and cleaning, as well as the work in the offices and on the wharves. But a private staircase leading from a cupboard into the merchant's private apartments bears witness to the fact that feminine company was smuggled in on occasions.

The apprentices were subject to a strict discipline. There was no bending of the rules for them, and fines and punishments were meted out for any disobedience, even for taking an extra sip more than the allotted half a litre of ale that was measured out at the communal meal. They were not allowed to enter the merchant's apartments, and had to make his wall-bed through a small aperture, the door of which was fastened from the inside and adorned with a pin-up painting of a charming lady of the day. The apprentices themselves slept head to toe in four cramped box-beds. They were usually the sons of rich Hanseats, and served four years' apprenticeship, afterwards being promoted to assistant, and finally becoming full-fledged merchants themselves. Evidence of a truly obsessional approach to business is there in the special lamps that were carried at the head of the funeral procession when any-one in the German community died, for as time was money to the Hanseats the dead were only buried at night out of trading hours!

In the museum hangs the oldest painting of Bergen, dated 1580, which shows the walled Hanseatic wharves of those days, the primitive cranes that dealt with the cargoes, and the carts that were pulled into the narrow passageways for loading and unloading. Fire was such a great hazard that all forms of heating were prohibited in Bryggen, even in the most bitter winters. It must have been a Spartan existence.

Also dating from medieval times is the church of St Jørgen (St George), formerly the church to the leper hospital. This latter was rebuilt after a fire in 1702 and now houses a leprosy museum, showing the devoted work of Norwegian doctors in their fight against the disease; it gives special honour to Armauer Hansen, the discoverer of the leprosy bacillus.

Bergen's little white gabled town hall has hardly changed since it was built in 1550 as a private residence for a Danish governor, Walckendorff. Although restoration did enlarge the building in the eighteenth century it is still too small for the 84 council members permitted by the Norwegian constitution, but rather than they should move out into other premises the Bergensers happily make do with fewer members, saying that 77 Bergenser councillors are equal to 84 anywhere else !

One of the most charming sections of the city is 'Old Bergen' where whole streets, alleys, and a market place, are preserved from the early nineteenth century. The wooden houses, which include the home of a prosperous Bergen sea-captain, are furnished in the period, and the shops, complete with hanging trade signs outside, are well stocked with the appropriate goods. Some scenes from the film *Song of Norway*, based on the life of Edvard Grieg, were filmed in Old Bergen.

It was Bergen's famous violinist, Ole Bull, who in 1858 encouraged the 15-year-old Edvard Grieg to go to the conservatoire in Leipzig, setting the young composer off on a path that was to take him far from Bergen before he returned to live there again, fired with a renewed and passionate love for his country and its folklore. The genius of Ole Bull, who died in 1880, lives on in the reputation that he gained during his lifetime when he gave concerts on both sides of the Atlantic, and was acclaimed as the greatest violinist ever born. In 1850 he founded Den Nationale Scene in Bergen, Norway's first theatre, which still flourishes today, and counts Henrik Ibsen and Bjørnstjerne Bjørnson among its great figures of the past.

Edvard Grieg's home is at Troldhaugen in the suburbs of Bergen. He lived there for the last 22 years of his life with his wife, Nina. It is a comfortable wooden villa painted green and white with a glass veranda and square tower, and it has been kept exactly as it was during his lifetime. It stands in peaceful isolation, surrounded by sun-dappled woodland, with a view of the unspoilt glittering Nordås lake; a path leads from the garden down to the rock where Norway's greatest composer lies interred with his wife. Down by the water's edge is the small pavilion where he composed some of his best-known works, inspired by the fjord country that he knew so well. There is his desk with his pen, inkwell, and the original manuscript of one of his compositions: it is as though he had risen from his chair only a few minutes before.

In the house hangs the famous portrait of Grieg as a young man, sitting with arms folded, his longish mane of hair and flowing moustache giving him a singularly contemporary appearance. Here again a feeling of his presence is heightened by the sight of his personal possessions amid all the plushy furniture, the lace curtains, and the chandeliers. His wide-brimmed grey hat hangs on a wall, and in the *salon* is the grand piano where he used to play while Nina stood by his side to sing. It was she who inspired him to write '*Jeg elsker deg*' ('I love thee'), and he wrote of her in a letter in 1900: 'She is for me the only one who can interpret my songs'.

During Bergen's annual International Festival of Music, Drama and Folklore, it is the highlight of the open-air morning recitals of Grieg's music at Troldhaugen when through the open windows his piano is heard again, the tones drifting out into the soft summer air.

Bergen has a long tradition of musical events, and its symphony orchestra, Musikselskabet Harmonien, with 65 members was founded in 1765, and is one of the oldest in the world. It recently passed its 200th season, and its concerts, often with world-famous conductors and soloists, attract music-lovers from far afield.

Appropriately in this city of music the railings of the observation platform on the top of Mount Fløien are wrought with quavers, semiquavers, and crotchets. The scarlet or blue funicular takes you up there, and leaves Bergen lying like a multi-coloured carpet far below. There are plenty of paths to follow on Mount Fløien that wander through woods and by lakes, and for those still feeling energetic it is a pleasant walk down to the streets again, past houses that lodge on the steep slopes, tucked away amid trees. An aerial view of Bergen and its environs can be had from the cable car that goes up 2,000 feet to Mount Ulriken, and there are paths for those who wish to wander off through the woods.

Among all that Bergen has to offer there is one place that should not be left out, and it is within easy reach by bus – or ten minutes on foot – from the centre of the city. It is the aquarium, said to be the finest anywhere in the world. It is situated on the Nordnes peninsula by the ten-storey Institute of Marine Research on what was once the site of a strong defence outpost – the Powder Magazine with its enormously thick walls still stands. The spot between the Aquarium's ticket office and the pond where the Greenland seal and the common seal cavort, now ornamented with a rock garden, was known in the past as Witches Hill, for it was here on the peninsula that Anne Persdotter and other witches were burnt at the stake.

When Queen Elizabeth II visited the aquarium with the two young princes on a visit to Bergen in 1969 other engagements that day were delayed as the children could not bear to leave the seals. The seal-pond is a never-ending source of entertainment and there is the additional pleasure of being able to watch them underwater from within the aquarium itself where suddenly all the outdoor, above-surface sounds are lost, and you are held in the air-bubbling silence akin to that in the depths of the sea.

The aquarium has access to all the clean sea-water it could possibly need, which is pumped from a depth so pure that it never needs filtering, its temperature and saline content remaining around the same level at all times of the year. The main room of the aquarium is designed like a great diving bell with nine windows looking out on a panorama of Norwegian marine life, each section under its own heading, such as 'The Cod Family', 'Beneath the Wharf', 'Sharks, Rays, and Conger Eels' and so on. The light makes even the army of humble herring appear as though sparkling with sequins, but the prima ballerina is without doubt the large silvery salmon.

A circular staircase leads down into a dark labyrinth that holds a seemingly endless chain of brightly illuminated pockets where a jewel-bright variety of sea-organs, species and individuals is followed in line of development from the most simple to the most complex. The whole aquarium has been built showing a special consideration for children and the tanks are angled for them, so that adults, although able to enjoy the display from their own height, will find that to stand back, or to bend down, is the best way to capture the truly superb view.

Outside again is the penguin pool. There the penguins squat and waddle along the rocks to stare with unblinking curiosity at the rows of faces looking down at them, almost as though they believed that the visitors were parading for their benefit!

Every evening the coastal steamers pass the aquarium on Nordnes Point as they leave Bergen for the far North. The round-voyage passengers are bound for 11 days of ever-changing scenery and 2,500 miles of sailing, sometimes up the fjords, sometimes across the mouth of them, always hugging the rugged coast, with the chance to go ashore at many ports along the way. It is all so arranged that places of importance missed during sleeping hours on the way up can be visited at a more convenient time on the way back. It is impossible to talk about night and day, for in the summer season there is nothing but daylight, the midnight sun making it possible to use a camera at any hour of the 24. And there is so much to photograph from Bergen to North Cape – Alesund of the herring fleets, the Rose-town of Molde, Mount Torghatten rising from the sea, said to be the hat of the Mountain King, the hole through it having been made by a great arrow; the city of Trondheim, the Lofoten Islands, Hammerfest, which is the most northerly town in the world, and a host of other places, all different, all in their own unique settings giving a full overall picture of Norway and the Norwegian way of life. And there is always the certificate issued to first-time passengers on the

authority of King Neptune in his realm of the midnight sun to prove that you have crossed the Arctic Circle at sea.

The arrival of these coastal steamers at even the smallest village port brings a cluster of people to the quayside, and sometimes a young people's brass band if it is a national holiday – children's bands are very popular and keen contests are held all over the country. As soon as the gangway is swung ashore, merchandise is despatched or collected, mailbags are heaved on or off, and people meet friends with much hand-shaking, or go abroad themselves, taking the steamer to another port as others might catch a bus.

It is possible to feel very involved in the everyday life that is going on around you. I remember a time when the steamer slowed to a standstill in mid-fjord to lower a special cradle over the side to pick up a small boy brought out by boat from a sea-locked farmstead. He had appendicitis, and at the next port an ambulance was waiting to whisk him off to hospital. In complete contrast there was the noisy, drunken merchant seaman, deliriously happy to be home again, and making a fine old uproar about it. He reeled down the gangway at his destination, and fell full length face downward on the snowy quay. A policeman came forward, helped him up and led him away, hidden by a rippling sweep of a cloak whirled about by the arm of the law with an ease that Dracula might have envied. Perhaps the merchant seaman was not as lucky as a man arrested for the 100th time for being drunk at Gjøvik: the police gave him coffee and cakes in acknowledgement of the record-breaking event.

Another coastal voyage to make is from Bergen round the southernmost tip of Norway and up to Oslo. This route was greatly used in the past before the first part of the Bergen–Oslo railway was laid down in 1883. It is a masterpiece of engineering; the building across difficult mountain terrain took almost half a century, the construction being hindered by severe climatic conditions at great heights, since much of the route passes through everlasting snow and ice. Two thousand men and 100 horses laboured and when winter came work was confined to the tunnels, but was

12 Fantoft stave church, near Bergen

made hazardous by falls and avalanches. Now the railway offers seven hours of scenery as widely varied as that which can be seen from the coastal steamers, for the route passes from the dramatic fjord landscape through eternal snows with immense glaciers to the softer, rolling countryside that encloses Oslo.

All seats are reserved on long-distance trains, and reservation is done only in Norway, so for the tourist travelling independently on a ticket purchased in his own country it is advisable to reserve a seat as far as possible in advance.

Stopover tickets are available for those who feel like breaking their journey; perhaps at Finse where Captain Scott trained his men and dogs for his South Pole expedition, or at Geilo, where in summer there are wonderful rambles among the hills that are full of dancing streams and quiet lakes. The chair-lift up to Mount Geilohøgda transports you to a wildly rugged moorland where trolls seem to peep behind every rock, and which in winter becomes the white slopes of a ski-resort.

Then there is the Flåm Line, which branches off at Myrdal at a height of 2,845 feet, and zigzags down for 12 miles to Flåm at sea-level on the Aurlandfjord, which is an arm of the great Sognefjord. It is a 45-minute journey of steep-sided, lush-green valleys, towering mountains caped in snow, and cascading water-falls. The guard gives a running commentary in both English and Norwegian, and the train obligingly stops twice – the first time for the benefit of photographers, who have been clicking and whirring all the time anyway, and the second time to allow everyone to get out at the foot of the thundering Kjøs waterfall. The knowledge that the carriages have five separate braking systems is comforting when at one point on the journey you see the line running at three different levels on the sharp mountainside and the train is still on the fourth one !

Like everything else in Norway the trains are spotlessly clean, and every now and again a uniformed cleaner will come along to sweep up any litter dropped by passengers too lazy to use the waste-bins provided. Trolleys of refreshments, both hot and cold, are wheeled along during long journeys, and this is in addition to the good food and service offered in the dining-car. Railway station restaurants keep up the same high standard. The train can become part of any holiday, linking up with coastal steamer or ferry, and for those who really like to do the whole thing on their own there is the highly organized internal jet airline to cut long distances, and the comfortable buses that take long journeys in their stride, timed in their turn to meet up with ferry, plane, and train.

I was on Bergen railway station one day when a party of young people were seeing a friend off on the first stage of a journey that was to take him by ship from Oslo to a research post in the United States. At the moment when the train started to move every one of them flung a rolled-up umbrella through the open window into his carriage – the traditional souvenir of Bergen. He waved one of those 32 umbrellas until he was lost from sight!

4. The Fjord Country

There is such peace in the fjord country. Sometimes the silence seems to assail the ear; at others the air is filled with the swirl of river, bubble of steam, and thunder of waterfall, punctuated by the tinkling of cowbells in the high pastures. Everywhere there are trim little villages and scattered farmsteads; many of the old buildings still have turf roofs from which small trees sprout like feathers in a hat, and flowers dip over the windows.

It is still a fairly common sight in the valleys on Saturday afternoons in summertime to see the farmers taking their Westland horses, high-prancing in excitement, up the slopes to set them loose in the mountains for the week-end, or until needed again. This is the reason why often a cluster of these gentle, creamy-coloured horses with the characteristic black streak through the mane and down the tail will come wandering up to you on their own in the mountains; yet when their patient owners come to call them down again they frequently make themselves scarce, appearing as pale specks against the high mountainsides where they are as sure-footed as any goat.

Another pretty sight is when a flock of sheep, all of which wander freely in the high pastures with their lambs throughout the summer, decide to take a trip home, perhaps a chill wind having reminded them of their cosy winter quarters under cover. With a jingling of bells they come from far away to stream down the slopes, follow the road and turn unerringly into their own farmstead. Then the farmer has to drop whatever he is doing to take them all the way up again. Occasionally a wild lynx or an eagle will take a lamb, but on the whole losses are few.

Indicative of the inherent honesty of the country-born Norwegian and his unshattered trust in his fellow-man are the little wooden signs that are sometimes found hanging by a front door in the farming districts; the carved arm of a troll, or simply a decorated indicator, will be pointing to an appropriate message among a variety that include: 'Gone shopping', 'Sleeping', 'Back in an hour', 'Back in ten minutes', and – surely the most trusting of all – 'Away on holiday' !

Each farm has its *stabbur*, the storehouse, the upper floor of which used to be an extra guest-room in days gone by, having the grandest furniture and hung with the best tapestries. Many of these stabburs have finely carved balconies and galleries, all in the long-held tradition that only the best was good enough for a guest. Nowadays guests are no longer put in the stabbur, but children love an excuse to sleep there when the house is full of company, for there is a certain enchantment about these quaint old buildings that smell of good corn stored on the lower floor, apples, meal, fermenting beer and home-made wine. Another feature of every country house, many town houses, all hotels, and almost all churches is the flag-staff. Having waited so many centuries for their own flag, the Norwegians now hoist the dark blue cross bordered with white on a brilliant scarlet field on every possible occasion. Its present form dates from 1821, but not until 1898 was the Norwegian flag shaken free of the special badge of union with Sweden that had clung to the upper left-hand corner. When there is a wedding in the village all the flags will fly, and in mourning all will be at half-mast. Outside mountain huts and holiday cottages nestled by the water the flags flutter, often simply in homage to yet another day being spent in the glories of nature.

The fjords change colour and mood with every turn of the weather, never becoming less of a feast for the eyes, not even when grey curtains of rain hiss across the water, for it is then that they take on a sombre, almost sinister grandeur, new waterfalls filling every gulley, veining the mountainside, adding their whiteness to the great cascades that come hurtling down, crashing over rock and boulder, throwing cold spume high into the air. On a quiet, damp day in Naerøyfjord wisps of mist hang veil-like between the rock cliffs that rise sheer on each side, and everything is black and purple and silvery-grey. At certain times in the Hardangerfjord near Ulvik the forest-clad slopes cause the water to take on the same rich hue, and it is as though you were viewing the whole scene through the clear green glass of a bottle.

Then there are those dazzling days when the wide fjords, such as Romsdal and Sogn, are full of sun-diamonds. That is when the mountains stand like blue-paper cutouts against an even bluer sky, and the rust, ochre, scarlet and cobalt buildings of the farmsteads and hamlets stand toy-bright on slopes where the corn is ripening. The drying hay, heaped on taut wires between poles, makes long feathery garlands all the way down to the water's edge where boats sail with their own inverted image, the ripples in their wake fanning out in arrow-heads across the turquoise surface.

Each fjord has its own characteristics, its own highlights, such as Lysefjord, which is famous for its 'Pulpit Rock' that soars up perpendicularly from the water to a height of 2,000 feet. From its flat 'pulpit' ledge there is a view across the county of Rogaland, where peak after peak of the Ryfylkeheiene stretch as far as the eye can see.

Lysefjord is within easy distance of Stavanger, the town that likes to be known as the Golden Key to the Fjords, for at regular intervals it is the first port of call for the ships of the Bergen Line coming from Newcastle. It has other links with Britain through its cathedral, which was built largely by English craftsmen brought across the North Sea to start work on it about 1125 by Bishop Reinald of Winchester, whose arm was for centuries a treasured relic in the care of the monks. Both Stavanger and Winchester Cathedrals have as their patron saint St Swithin, Bishop of Winchester, who went on a pilgrimage to Rome with Alfred the Great and died in the year 862.

The cathedral holds much of interest, in particular the beautiful baroque pulpit, carved in wood by Andrew Smith in 1682, who set in vividly-coloured biblical scenes and ornamented the crown-like canopy with a host of musical angels and winged cherubs.

Below the cathedral is the market-place, a central point that radiates out into broad avenues with starkly designed shops and offices, making a sharp contrast to the narrow medieval lanes of rounded cobblestones that wander between squat, wooden houses, painted in soft colours, that seem to have risen up from the pages of a book of fairy tales. In a main street not far from Lake Breia-vatnet, well-favoured by swans that have taken a liking to the salt-rimed town, is the local royal residence, Ledål Manor, which was built in 1800 and can be visited at certain hours.

Stavanger is wholly dedicated to the sea, thriving on ship-building and fish-canning, a busy, prosperous place that is a sea-food gourmet's paradise. Here can be had some of the best lobsters ever tasted, and restaurants offer a choice of fish still swimming about in tanks that form part of the décor. The International Sea Fishing Festival is held in August, but visitors can go deep-sea fishing any time in the summer on the arrangement of 'No catch, no cash', which makes a wonderful family outing.

It was at Hafrsfjord near Stavanger that in 872 a decisive battle of Viking ships took place. Harald Fairhair emerged as victor, and became king of all Norway. He lived to be 80, and chose as his last resting-place a spot close to Haugesund, not far from where the great victory was won. Haugesund is one of the largest shipping towns in Norway, and is within excursion distance of Stavanger, the ferry passing between islands. There an obelisk, raised by the townspeople in 1872 to commemorate the 1,000th anniversary of unification, shows up on the skyline at the place where Harald Fairhair lies under a huge block of stone that was of his own choos-ing. He had abdicated three years before his death, handing Nor-way over into the care of one of his many sons, Eirik Bloodaxe, who unfortunately lived up to his ferocious name.

From Haugesund, as from Stavanger, routes lead deep into the county of Hordaland. Among all the waterfalls that tumble and cascade the two-channelled Låtefoss is one of the most spectacular. It thunders down a full 540 feet, so that a permanent mist hung with rainbows drifts over the road where tourists make jokes about getting a free car-wash, and buy postcards of it at the kiosk to send home. From Låtefoss the road continues on by the side of Sørfjord, an arm of the most romantic of all the fjords, Hardanger.

In May the whole district lies under a settled cloud of pink and white fruit blossom, and the drifting petals catch in the lush grass and float away on the fjord. Hardanger has so many hamlets and villages where it is possible to be tucked away from all traffic in complete retreat amid surroundings of majestic beauty that can be explored on foot, in boats, and with fishing-rod and binoculars. As all over Norway, there are *pensjonats* and *gjestgiveris* in which to stay when a place is too small to have an hotel, and although accommodation is simple and the menu limited they are always spotlessly clean. *Overnatting* and *Rum* are signs that offer the simplest accommodation of all, and mean what they say: overnight and room in a private house, but no food provided, although sometimes the additional sign of *Kjøkken* (kitchen) means that facilities are available for making a pot of coffee and cooking yourself a meal. These will be cheap, but with the same high standards of cleanliness, although the plumbing can be a little strange in out-of-the-way places. Then there are the camping huts where you must have your own sleeping bag, but each hut contains an electric plate for cooking, saucepans and a kettle. Some of these sites with the beds made up are called 'motels' by their owners, so unless a motel is starred on your tourist chart it is wise to check on the accommodation before booking in, for to the average tourist the word 'motel' is synonymous with a great deal of comfort and a T.V. in the bedroom, particularly if you have stayed in the luxurious motels of Sweden and Finland.

There are also the weekend and holiday huts belonging to individual Norwegian families; this accommodation is entirely different as you will be walking into a miniature home in the mountains, on an island, or on the coast. They have to be booked months in advance, but in their idyllic settings they offer the kind of peaceful holiday that every Norwegian loves, for it is as necessary for him to commune with nature as it is for him to take food and drink, a fact that was remarked upon by an R.A.F. officer who was posted through N.A.T.O. to a Norwegian air force base. He was surprised to find the mess empty when he went in for a sociable hour before dinner. 'Where is everybody?' he asked the barman. 'They've all gone walking on their own in the mountains', was the reply, 'but they'll be back for dinner.' The same pattern was repeated every evening. 'The mountains are there', a Norwegian pilot explained patiently to the officer, 'and it would be a waste not to walk up them at least once a day.'

In his time Edvard Grieg was no exception in wanting to be in the mountains, and at Lofthus, surrounded by Hardanger's magnificence, is the tiny log hut where he spent summer holidays and composed some of his best-known works, capturing the sounds of the mountains, rivers, and waterfalls that inspired him on all sides. A return boat trip, taking six hours there and back, from Lofthus to the village of Norheimsund, gives the chance to view Hardanger from the water. Norheimsund is small and picturesque with rambling narrow streets and a waterfall, which descends like a shining veil, that you can walk under.

At Ullensvang the spire of the little medieval church rises above the fruit blossom to soar against the distant backcloth of the Folgefonnen glacier in one of the most-photographed Hardanger views. There is Ulvik at the head of a small arm of the fjord, sometimes approached by the old post-road, and Kinsarvik where once the dragon heads of the Viking ships bobbed alongshore – the remains of a Viking boat-house can still be seen. On the wide expanse of the Hardanger plateau thousands of wild reindeer roam, and frequently cross the roads in a forest of antlers.

Hardanger is renowned for its crown-weddings. For a long time these had become a rare sight, but in recent years many young people, particularly if they belong to a folk-dancing club or any folklore association, have chosen to revive and keep alive many of the old customs. These crown-weddings are so-called because the bride will top the colourful finery of her national costume with the traditionally ornate, heavily-decorated gold or silver wedding crown, which may have been in the possession of her family for centuries. These crowns are to be seen in the museums, aglitter with tier after tier of finely-wrought droplets, but unfortunately many of them were lost and melted down during the years of Danish domination to pay the heavy silver tax imposed by the Danes.

Brides in white will sometimes hire a lighter version of the wedding crown from goldsmiths, which is in the high-pointed style of the type that the fairy-tale princess is always wearing in the final illustration in the story-book when the prince leads her off on a white horse towards the distant castle. In the old days brides did ride to church on horseback, resplendent in their wedding regalia, and to this day fiddlers escort the traditional bride to church, and after the ceremony lead the whole wedding procession to the place where the reception is to be held. In Hardanger it is always the old Hardanger fiddle that is played, which resounds splendidly in the open air for it produces a full-volumed droning polyphonic music. Its origins are lost in time, but it could have evolved from the string instruments that the Vikings used, for something of their art lingers in the ornamentation on the earliest fiddles made by local Hardanger craftsmen, who became renowned for their skill in the eighteenth century.

In the past a bride always had a wedding chest, beautifully decorated in rococo style and incorporating garlands of flowers, ribbons and leaves. Her single name would be added on the side, together with the year of the wedding; in it she would pack all the linen she had woven, her new clothes, silverware and other possessions, and it went with her to her new home. These chests, as well as the earlier, plainer ones, have become heirlooms, greatly treasured and impossible to buy. They can be seen in museums, and have a place of honour on display in private homes as well as in many of the hotels that are furnished in traditional style. Sometimes a bride today will receive a new chest as a gift, and being hand-made it will be very costly, an antique of the future. The 'rose-painting' that ornaments so attractively so much antique furniture, sometimes whole ceilings in an ancient farmhouse fortunate enough to have escaped redecoration, is part – with the making of fiddles – of a great burst of peasant art in the seven-teenth and eighteenth centuries, and often even the humblest cooking-spoon of that time will have the most carefully painted design running down the handle.

At Voss, one of the country's largest tourist resorts, also in the county of Hordaland, it can almost be guaranteed that every Saturday will see a traditional wedding procession escorted to and from the thirteenth-century church in the centre of the town. Not only the bride and groom, but most of the guests as well will be in national costume. After dinner the merriment may go on to the early hours; coffee and cakes are served later, and the wedding cake is the traditional tall pyramid of almond rings decorated with tiny Norwegian flags, miniature crackers, sugar flowers, and topped by a bride and groom.

In Voss on Midsummer Eve, which is celebrated all over Nor-way with bonfires in the old pagan festival in honour of the *solsnu*, the turn of the sun, children process through the town, all in their bright national costumes, enacting a rustic wedding in miniature to the great delight of proud local mothers and camera-happy tourists. Just a short uphill walk west of the station is one of the oldest secular buildings in the country, the richly black-timbered Finneloft, which was used as a banqueting hall in medieval times. The cable-car, used by skiers when Voss takes on its winter role as a leading ski-resort, climbs to a height of 2,200 feet, giving a tremendous view of the town, the shining lake, and the mountains all around. For those who wish to go higher still a chair-lift from there completes a rise to almost 3,000 feet on Mount Hangar.

From Voss there are two equally spectacular routes to follow to Sognefjord. A pin stuck in a map can decide the issue, and the left-out one can be saved for the next time. Firstly there is the road that climbs by way of Stalheim with its eye-feasting view that includes the 1,150-feet-deep wooded ravine, also the famous Jorsdalsnuten, the mountain that rises like a giant thimble, and the Naerøy valley that spreads out in a flower-dusty carpet of green and gold. Then the steepest road in Norway descends by

way of 13 hairpin bends, the 414 feet perpendicular drop of the
Stalheim Falls and the white cascade of the Sivle Falls giving
added splendour. It was at this point that I once saw an American
tourist, running out of film in his enthusiasm, slam his camera
back on to the coach seat, and exclaim furiously: 'There's too
much darned scenery in this country!'

Throughout Norway, and of particular advantage in these districts, are the picnic tables and benches that are set up off the road
for the convenience of travellers, usually where a view can be
seen at its best. Made of rough wood or hewn stone, the picnic
tables blend into their settings: the Stalheim Falls can be viewed
from such a spot.

The road passes on to reach the ferry for Kaupanger from
Gudvangen, where the hotel has a framed advertisement for one of
Cook's first tours in Norway. It was at this spot that in the past a
fleet of 500 wagonettes would wait to take the passengers from
cruise ships up into the mountains to admire the views. My husband remembers when open cars gathered at these spots in the
thirties, and the excitement of these occasions for the local children. As a small boy he used to gaze in wide-eyed amazement at
the Englishmen in their tweed caps and vast plus-fours, strange
garments to Norwegian eyes at that time; all the ladies tied scarves
over their cloche hats and were tucked in with motoring rugs. In
fair weather and foul they were all driven in those open cars up
into the heights.

The other route from Voss is across the Vikafjell, a mountainous way that is my favourite of the two, because I always look
forward to the view of Vik in Sogn that comes from a great height.
There the village lies in a curved saucer of farmland, clustered at
the head of an arm of the peacock-coloured fjord with range after
range of mountains lumbering away in the distance on the far side
of the water. The road descends in bends, and there comes into
sight, set in quiet solitude, the pagoda-roofed stave church of
Hopperstad, much less visited than those in more easily accessible
areas, and often missed among the trees by those not alerted to
look out for it. A rough country lane leads to it, and as soon as you

draw near a housewife from a near-by farm comes hurrying down with a gigantic key to open it up for you. (Unfortunately not all the key-keepers are so alert, and it is disappointing to find so many of the beautiful little country churches locked against you. But *somebody* near by will have the key, and an inquiry at the local shop or hotel soon brings results.)

Like the prow of the Oseberg ship in Oslo the west portal of the Hopperstad Church is heavily carved with winged beasts and serpents entwined together in mortal combat, which is not such a coincidence, for in Vik (which means bay), as in so many similar places, the skilled local craftsmen would have worked on both the church and the Viking ships, employing similar designs on both ecclesiastical and sea-going timbers. Even the choir screen has the look and feel of a ship's beams, and one of the three altars has a canopy with carved sculpted heads like an inverted boat.

Unfortunately at some time the richly painted medieval paintings on the walls were scraped away, and only a few traces remain. Yet the fact that the church itself survives today is due to the intervention of an architect, Peter Blix, who saved it from destruction in the mid nineteenth century. He also stepped in to save from demolition the near-by Hove Church, which dates from the same time, and is the oldest stone building in Sogn, buying it outright and restoring it at his own expense. He is buried in Hove Church, and the district owes much to this man, whose epitaph reads: 'For the love of Art he raised again this House of God.' In 1969 it was discovered that the old bells from Hove Church, bought in Amsterdam in 1690, and sent abroad before Peter Blix could save them, were hanging in a mission in Madagascar. New bells were sent to replace them, and the Hove bells were returned to Vik.

The road from Vik is cut into the wooded mountainside and runs at the water's edge round to Vangnes where, according to the sages, Fridtjof the Bold lived. The German Kaiser, Wilhelm II of the fierce eyes and bristling moustache who used to cruise in his yacht on the fjords, had erected in 1913 a gigantic statue of Fridtjof, which looms rather incongruously above the hamlet of Vangnes like a petrified Gulliver. The face is more Gothic-German

than Norse, and the gaze is rather oddly turned away from the
wide expanse of fjord where his ships would have set sail. From
Vangnes the ferry crosses to Balestrand, which was one of the
Kaiser's favourite ports of call.

Balestrand is difficult to beat for sheer scenic magnitude. It is
impossible to resist the breath-taking setting, for Balestrand is
situated on a promontory in the fjord, backed by mountains, with
vistas across the fjord whichever way you turn, and a glacier
thrown in for good measure. No wonder the Kaiser used to feast
his eyes for hours from the balcony of the Kvikne Hotel, which
stands with a kind of wedding-cake elegance, white and wooden
and drenched in charm, reflected deep in the placid water.

Continuing north you come, by way of some roller-coaster roads
through forests and by lakes, to the village of Olden that lies at the
head of the innermost arm of Nordfjord, not far from Jostedal, the
largest glacier in Europe, and the second largest in the world,
stretching all the way from Sognefjord to Nordfjord. For the truly
energetic in the right footwear a walk across the glacier can be
arranged, but it must never be attempted without an experienced
guide. Many fatal accidents have resulted when people have tried
it on their own. In fact, if in any doubt about going into the mountains at any time, ask the advice of local people and take it.

I remember well the time a young Danish couple set off to climb
some tricky terrain in the face of bad weather against the advice
of the owner of a small café where they had stopped for coffee. He
became increasingly anxious as he watched for them and they
failed to return. Finally he raised the alarm. In terrible wind and
weather the men of the village searched all night, helped by tourist
climbers anxious to assist. Dawn was breaking when a Danish
youth in the search-party remarked in exhaustion that he had had
no idea that such a storm had been brewing, and if he hadn't had
a row with his girl-friend the two of them would also have been
stranded on some ledge. A silence fell. Everybody looked at him.
'A row? Didn't you return together?' someone asked with tight-
lipped control. He stared round in dismay at the faces of the
search-party as comprehension crashed home. It was he himself

for whom they had all been searching, and for his girl-friend, who was tucked up asleep at the *pensjonat*. It came out that they had quarrelled about the advice given. The girl-friend had taken it, turning back almost at once, and two hours later, having decided it would be better to patch things up, the young Dane returned, and was spotted in the distance by the café-owner, who had thought he was just another solitary climber getting home like all the others in good time. The newspapers reported gleefully the story of the Dane who had searched all night for himself!

A popular excursion from Olden is a ride in one of the wagonettes, drawn by sturdy little Westland horses, up to see Briksdalbreen, which is an arm of the Jostedal glacier, shimmering like ice-cream in the sun. The horses clip-clop at a leisurely pace until they reach the enormous waterfall where they almost gallop across the bridge as the icy spume, shot with rainbows, swirls over it. Above the great cascade the ride becomes gentle again to the clearing where everyone gets out to follow on foot the path that leads up the rocks to the lake at the foot of the glacier. The water sweeps out from a sapphire cave in the ice, and even in the hottest summer small icebergs float glittering across the deep blue surface.

Not far away from Olden is Loen of the wild and beautiful turquoise lake. It was here that in 1936 a great avalanche fell into the lake, causing a tidal wave that swept inland. Seventy-four people lost their lives, and whole farmsteads were carried down into the depths of the green-blue water. An earlier disaster in 1905 took 60 lives.

In Nordfjord, as in other parts of Norway, mountain farms perch on the rugged slopes, often with a tiny handkerchief of arable land, amazing those who see them for the first time. Many of these isolated farmsteads can only be reached by boat across the fjord, or perhaps by an overland route that no car could use. 'How on earth can those people make a living?' is the most common question. In the past a man could bring up a family and scrape an existence on such a farm. He would have a few sheep, some goats, and a cow. There was timber on his land and fish in the sea. It was a hard life, but he was his own master. Now nobody wants to husband those farms any more, but they have never been in greater demand and are impossible to buy on the open market, for they make the most wonderful holiday homes, and Norwegians keep them furnished with antique peasant furniture whenever possible.

I have stayed on a mountain farm not far from Nordfjordheid, known as Grøthaug (which means Porridge Hill). It got its name from the distant past when the women of the farm used to take cream porridge, known as *rømme grøt*, to the men working on the high slopes there. They carried the porridge in special wooden containers with a lid which a peg kept fastened, always gaily decorated with a pattern. *Rømme grøt* is very rich, made almost entirely of cream, and the golden fat that bubbles out of it is spooned to one side and served separately with cinnamon and sugar to sprinkle over the porridge. In the past it was filling, everyday fare, but in the lean years it was reserved for special occasions, such as the end of haymaking and when the harvest had been brought safely in. It made a gift to a new mother, 'bed food' being enough food provided by the other women in the neighbourhood to keep the husband and the rest of the children well fed until the mother was able to cope again. Today it is still a luxury but for another reason: diet-conscious Norwegians, being only too aware of its fattening qualities and its high cholesterol content, eat it only when allowing themselves a special treat. It is served in museums, cafeterias, restaurants, and appears in those meals laid on as traditional fare for the tourists on a folklore evening, who often misjudge it by its semolina appearance, declaring they do not like it at the first spoonful. Admittedly it is an acquired taste, but I thought its rich creaminess delicious from the moment I first tasted it.

Grøthaug has changed little since those early 'porridge hill' days, and the traditional hospitality is the same. At a farm breakfast it is not unusual to have as many as 30 assorted dishes of food on the table, including cold meats, a variety of cheeses, boiled eggs, stewed fruit, bowls of fresh berries, waffles (always heart-shaped), smoked salmon and various other kinds of fish, home-

13   A corner of Vik stave church (see frontispiece)

made preserves, home-baked bread and rolls, and even cakes, together with jugs of both fresh and specially-soured milk, all rounded off by superb coffee.

These huge breakfasts are laid out on a central table in all the hotels for guests to help themselves as often as they wish, but it is as well to check which of the jugs contains the soured milk, for there is nothing worse than discovering that you have poured it by mistake on your cornflakes! Beware, also, the *gammel ost* (old cheese), which is dark and quite pleasant in appearance, but there is always a glass cover over it, and when it is lifted you will know the reason why!

My late mother-in-law was born at Grøthaug, and she often talked to me of her early childhood, conjuring up a picture of a way of life that had been practically unchanged through the centuries, but has now gone for ever. She had to go all the way down the mountainside to school, whatever the weather. Neither rain nor blizzard stopped the whole family from walking the long distance each way on Sundays to attend church at Nordfjordheid. It was even farther up to the farm's *saeter*, a group of huts and byres in the high mountain pastures where the daughters of farm families lived all summer, tending the cattle there, making butter and cheese, and sending the milk down in churns on taut wires evening and morning to be collected below by the dairy carts. In those days every farm had its saeter, but today very few are still used for the purpose for which they were built, having become in turn the perfect holiday cabin in the mountains.

My mother-in-law's brothers were among the many thousands that emigrated to the United States and Canada at the turn of the century, following an earlier wave in the 1860s, which has resulted in there being as many Norwegian–Americans on the other side of the Atlantic as there are people in Norway. A treasured relic far away in Seattle is a spinning-wheel made by great-grandfather Grøthaug, who had been taught in his youth the handed-down skill of generations past in making them. Today Grøthaug spinning-wheels are collectors' pieces.

One of Inge's earliest memories is of going to the wedding of an

14, 15   A farmhouse and a room in the Folk Museum, Nolde

uncle at Grøthaug. He travelled with his father and mother, six brothers and sisters, all of whom were under the age of twelve, in a wagonette from Tresfjord in Romsdal, complete with a large hamper of food for the long journey. They drove over the mountains to Vaksvik where they took a boat to Straumshamn. There a taxi-car with yellow celluloid windows, making it almost impossible to see out, took the whole crowd to the top of a mountain where Uncle Stefan Grøthaug met them with a horse and cart for the last lap of two-and-a-half hours' duration to Grøthaug farm. They arrived at 7 a.m., having travelled a full 24 hours. Rolf, one of the brothers, was first out of the cart. He dashed forward on a lightning tour of exploration, flung open the door of a well, and promptly fell in head first!

This journey to a wedding illustrates how in the 1930s travel in Norway was still far from easy, but how much more difficult it must have been before that. No wonder when people gathered together from far and wide for any kind of social event it was liable to go on for several days, often as long as a week. Guests were put up in all the neighbouring farms, resulting in the involvement of a whole valley in the occasion. This tradition survives in many parts of Norway today when someone from every farm will be invited to a wedding, and although the celebrations nowadays only last from the ceremony to the early hours of the next day, it is a costly affair, a minimum of three meals being laid on for as many as 200–300 guests. Between courses at the main feast, and in addition to the speeches, there are songs, the words of which will have been written specially for the occasion by the bride and groom and their respective families and friends, and are sung by all to well-known tunes. There is the bride's thanks to her parents; the best man's tribute to the groom; the bride's sister's account of the romance, and so on. Often witty, usually humorous, and sometimes touching, these songs are saved as souvenirs of the happy day.

The local involvement in each other's lives has resulted in a strong community spirit, and in the past even annual domestic chores, such as salting and curing meat after the slaughtering, or the making of *flatbrød* (a paper-thin bread that keeps crisp indefinitely), brought the women of the valleys together in small groups to help each other. I was lucky enough to be present at the last communal baking of flatbrød ever held at Øvstedal. About 20 housewives had gathered in the old bakehouse attached to the farm, and while some mixed the dough, the others rolled it out with patterned rolling-pins to the size of large dinner-plates; then those in charge of the baking flicked up the prepared 'plates', and crisped them golden on vast gridirons. With pots of coffee and chatter, and a great deal of merriment, the day flew past, and the chore of making the traditional 'flat bread' for the whole winter had been completed in a party atmosphere. Now the homemade flatbrød rarely appears, but the commercially made and packaged product has become as familiar on the supermarket shelves in Britain and other countries as it is in Norway.

On the coast near the mouth of Nordfjord is the village of Maløy, set at the foot of high wooded slopes, which became well known during World War II when, in December 1941, Allied commandos made a surprise attack on the Germans there, and fierce fighting took place in the narrow streets between the little boxy houses. It is one of the many interesting ports of call of the coastal steamers, which sail on from there towards Stad, catching a glimpse of the Alfot glacier, and then on past the island of Selje where King Olav Trygvasson had a church built and dedicated to St Sunniva, the patron saint of West Norway. She was a Christian princess from Ireland, who had perished there in a cave, trapped by an avalanche that had come between her and the pagans pursuing her. The legend tells that when the cave was finally opened she was as beautiful and serene in death as she had been in life.

To the centre of Nordfjord is Stryn, and a scenic road meets the Reindeer Road at Grotli, which links Lom in the east to Geiranger in the west. Once fog was so thick here that we drove from Lom to Geiranger without seeing the large hotel at Grotli where we had intended to stop. It was a nightmare ride. Clear patches in the fog revealed the sheer drop at the edge of the narrow

road to the frozen lake below where broken ice had refrozen in
the exceptionally cold spell to form jagged points that stood up
like the blue-white fangs of a troll. That has been my only experience of really bad fog in the mountains, but it is one of the
hazards when driving at great heights as often whole clouds will
swathe the road in white mist. Ever since that time Grotli has
made up for it with excellent weather, allowing me to bask bliss-
fully in the July sunshine while watching the slalom and downhill
racing of the Fjord Ski Festival on the snow-covered slopes of the
Jostedal glacier. On the same day I have gone up the toll road of
Nibbeveien, which leads off the Reindeer Road, to Mount
Dalsnibba at 4,590 feet to look in the other direction over the wide
map-like appearance of the rugged terrain to the blue patch that
is Geirangerfjord, where the water-skiing events of the same
festival take place.

Geiranger is Norway's most dramatic fjord. Its sides are too
steep and sheer for any habitation, but are hung with tufts of wild
plants and flowers, and laced by waterfalls. The road zigzags
down, and the observation layby reveals the whole sweep of
Flydals gorge, over which a great rock juts pulpit-shaped with a
breath-taking drop, down to Geiranger village at the head of the
fjord.

The road continues to wind down to the village, and then along
the water's edge to twist upwards again as the famous Eagle Road.
Each hairpin bend lets Geiranger fall a little farther away, giving
views round the mountain cliffs to where the Seven Sisters waterfall tumbles down into the curving fjord. A cruising liner is as
tiny as a free plastic model out of a cornflakes packet, and a mere
dot making triangular ripples on the blue-glass water is the ferry
passing by.

After the Eagle Road you are soon in a wildly rocky landscape
that is full of goats. Cream and grey, russet, tan, and ginger, they
lodge like china ornaments in every nook and cranny on the
mountainsides. Woe betide the car-driver who stops to get out and
take a photograph when a particularly appealing herd blocks the
road! As soon as he and his family emerge – for children are

always enchanted by the dainty little kids – the goats flock from all directions to form a sea of horns and round bright eyes, all of them eager for the cakes and sandwiches, and perhaps a taste of delicious tobacco, which long experience has taught them to expect. Their manners are appalling. They are quite without patience. They push into the car, jump on the seats and refuse to come out, while others put scratchy hooves on the shining paint-work to peer into the boot when it is opened for the tin of biscuits or the picnic hamper. My advice when you see a herd is to draw up and wait for the next car that comes along. Tourists are always caught by the goats. Behind glass you can have all the fun without getting involved yourself, or having to clean out the car after a goat invasion.

Goats are important in Norway and their cheese appears on almost every Norwegian table, a pleasing dark caramel colour with a sweetish taste. Sliced neatly with that most sensible of Norwegian inventions, the cheese 'plane' or slicer, it is particularly delicious on thickly buttered rye bread . (The cheese slicer was, incidentally, the brainchild of a poor carpenter, Thor Bjørklund, who in 1915 found it an economical way to make the cheese go round on the bread of his many children. It was an idea that made his fortune.)

The road descends to Eidsdal where the ferry leaves for Overåneset and Linge. The ferries all over Norway are so up to date and efficient that the service they offer cannot be bettered anywhere. As a safety precaution car- and coach-passengers have to get out during the driving of vehicles on and off the ferries, and to see cars disembark at the height of the tourist season is a riot akin to a Keystone comedy. The cars roll off ahead of their passengers, who always – without exception, and for no reason at all ! – follow at a breakneck run. They all do it. I do it myself. The rush to be in the car and away is infectious. People hurl themselves in with their driver, and car-doors slam as engines accelerate. It resembles the start of a car-rally every time, and all quite pointless, for most roads – by the very nature of the terrain – restrict all haste. Driving in the mountains is of a very high standard, Norwegians being particularly courteous, always quick to reverse to a passing place, marked with an 'M', when meeting a foreign car on a narrow way. The yellow and black *Vei-Patrole* cars patrol the high mountain roads to help any motorist in difficulties. I remember the nervous Frenchwoman, who on meeting a large bus on a narrow zigzag road leapt out of her car and gave way to hysterics. The *Vei-Patrole* man soothed her down, reversed her car for her, and drove her out of those particular hairpin bends.

Disembarking at Linge, after a ferry-ride past sharply rising, tree-covered slopes where mountain farms perch precariously, is to come to Sylte mountain where the shape of a serpent is clearly defined. Legend has it that King Olav the Holy, Norway's patron saint, battled with it when he came there in 1028, and hurled it to its death against the mountain wall. There are so many places in Norway where strange and beautiful formations of rock and land are attributed to his holy actions; a gorge is where St Olav ran his sword through the mountain, and narrow sounds show where the solid rock parted before the prow of his ship to let him through. The trolls that lived in the caves and shadows feared his might, but tried to trick him with some evil mischief wherever he went. Yet he was a match for them every time, and his way through Norway is marked by the trolls that he turned to stone, still standing cowed and huddled on the same spots today.

From the place of the serpent the road rises leisurely to the great height of Trollstigen, Ladder of the Trolls. In this wild landscape it is easy to imagine the presence of those strange creatures. Stories of the trolls have scared and delighted throughout the centuries, and it is small wonder that sometimes they seem very real when every mountain holds thousands of petrified troll faces in the rock. Trolls come in all sizes: some have three heads, some as many as five; others are as big as mountains or as small as a hazel nut, and lots of them have long, long noses ornamented with a growing tree. They have a penchant for beautiful maidens, liking to carry them away into their mountain caves, but on the whole they are slow-thinking and easily outwitted by human beings.

At Trollstigen in June the snow still banks the road at a height of 20 feet or more, and the international giant slalom competition, known as the 'Troll Ski Race' is held there. The crowds of spectators that gather there to watch the events refresh themselves in the hot sunshine with ice-cream purchased from vendors who carry their insulated boxes slung over one shoulder. The snow is crisp, sparkling and hard enough to walk on in stout shoes. Many spectators come prepared to ski themselves between events, and the prettiest girls wear bikinis, shooting about on their skis, sun-goggles flashing, pale hair streaming.

Just below Trollstigen the rushing river gathers itself for the 600-feet drop into the valley below. The bridge over it could easily be the one that the three goats crossed when they outwitted the river-troll lurking in the water, who had fancied them for his supper. From the bridge a path leads to Stigrøra, which gives a view of the Trollstig road that loops in 11 hairpin bends down the mountainside, crossing half-way down the thundering force of the Stig waterfall and looking very much like a roll of grey ribbon that has been cast down by some giant troll hand.

The village of Åndalsnes with its *Velkommen* (welcome) archway gives the first glimpse of the Romsdal fjord. Dominating the Romsdal Alps that enclose the village and the majestic gorge full of waterfalls is the blunt-crowned Romsdal Horn up which guides will take climbers. In the Rauma river there is good salmon fishing, and it was here that Prince Philip and Prince Charles fished during their informal visit to Norway in 1969. A nearby arm of the fjord is Isfjord where at the spot called Skothammer (Scots Cliff) 300 Scottish mercenaries under the leadership of Colonel Ramsay and Captain Sinclair landed in 1612 to march through the mountains to give aid to Sweden in one of her many wars against Norway and Denmark. The monument on Klungnes Farm there was raised to the memory of Per Klungnes, a farmer who was forced to act as their guide but who used his wits to make them take a long detour around Isfjord to Åndalsnes while one of his servants took a short cut to raise the alarm. By the time the Scots reached Åndalsnes the people had been alerted all along the route they

were to take up Romsdal gorge and into Gudbrandsdal. All the
young men were away fighting, but the peasants who were left –
the elderly, the young, and the women – banded together to wipe
the Scots out successfully with an ambuscade at Kringen in
Gudbrandsdal.

Not far from Åndalsnes is Eikesdal where until 1970 there fell
unchallenged the highest waterfall in Europe, Mardalsfoss. Then
plans were put into action to harness the water-power for use in
Romsdal. Not only did the conservationists rise up in anger, but
the Eikesdal folk objected strongly to their great loss being Romsdal's gain. The television news crackled with opinions given for
and against. 'We've so many waterfalls,' one man stated solidly,
'nobody is going to miss just one.' But that was not the opinion of
hundreds of people who staged a peaceful sit-down demonstration
in the path of the bulldozers taking part in the building of the road
to where the power-plant was to be erected. Conservationists and
people from Eikesdal chained themselves to rocks, and it was all
very exciting and unusual for Norway. Finally it was the coming
of snow that forced the protesters to disperse. A mountain top in
an arctic temperature is no place for a sit-down demonstration.

Romsdalsfjord is as much as six miles wide in places, and full of
small islands where it is possible to picnic all alone. On them all the
seabirds nest, and pay little attention to fires of crackling twigs
lighted to cook fish already caught and set a coffee-pot steaming.
One island, called Gjermundnes Holmen, off the village of
Vikebukt, is the burial place of one of the many Viking kings who
ruled in this district before the unification of Norway. The sun-
shot water is so clear that before the fjord plunges to its great
inner depths it is possible to see the quick flick of darting fish and
the slightly spectral jellyfish wafting by.

Sweeping out of the Romsdalsfjord is Tresfjord, and the road
mounts to a vantage point where the whole of its great cul-de-sac
of mountains with the green scooped-out valley makes a background to the little octagonal Tresfjord church, the heart of the
farming community that lies at the head of the tributary. It was rebuilt in 1828, its wooden walls painted white, and inside it is

decorated by peasant hands of the past in a riot of pattern. The splendidly primitive altar was carved in the seventeenth century by a local craftsman, Sjur Iversen Skjegstad, whose payment for the work was three barrels of corn.

My son was baptized in this church and I have also attended a confirmation there. Confirmation in Norway is a turning point in life akin to coming of age, all being confirmed at the age of 15 and considering themselves fully adult from that time forward. Family parties, together with the giving of large cards and lavish gifts, follow the service at which all the candidates wear white gowns over their new clothes and are required to answer in turn a question put to them on the teaching they have received, which is something of an ordeal for even the most brash teenager in the silence of the listening congregation. People often date early happenings in their lives as being before or after confirmation, and sometimes introduce a friend with the additional information 'we were confirmed together'. Dating from the sixteenth century the Evangelical Lutheran Church has been the established form of worship, counting 96 per cent of the population as confirmed members, but church attendance in general is the same as in any other European country.

Near Tresfjord Church is the dairy that produces a particularly good local cheese called Ridderost (Knights Cheese), which has a pleasant texture and piquant taste and is exported all over the world.

One small part of the Tresfjord valley is known as Rypdal, a name that goes back to the time of the Black Death when – as in so many other places in Norway – the whole community was wiped out, except that here one woman had survived. For a long time she believed herself to be the last person left alive in the land, for the bubonic plague had left the fjord silent and bereft of all boats. Then one day she saw a man coming over the mountains, and screamed out in delirious joy at seeing another human being. He, not seeing her, thought her scream was only that of the *ryper* (ptarmigan) and would have gone on his way if she had not pursued him to make her presence known. The place where she

cried to him has been known as Rypdal, Ptarmigan Valley, ever
since.

The road continues on to Ålesund, a way to take time over as
the views are ever-changing. At Sjøholt apricots and peaches are
grown out of doors, giving some idea of the strength of summer in
this northern clime, and then comes the salty town of Ålesund
itself, which is Norway's largest fishing town. Trawlers hung with
nets, festooned with floats bright as oranges, bob around every
corner. If you decide to go deep-sea fishing yourself the hotel where
you are staying will obligingly cook and serve your catch, which is
extremely satisfying. For years one of the sights to see in Ålesund
has been the giant rock in the centre of the town where hundreds
of seagulls perch and nest with a fine disregard for the traffic passing close by. They also land with the same careless indifference on
the statue raised to Kaiser Wilhelm II, who favoured Ålesund as
another of his ports of call on his cruising holidays, and who after
a disastrous fire in 1904 donated generously towards the rebuilding. Within boat-trip range is Runde, an island that is a sanctuary
for half a million sea-birds, including some rare species.

The best place from which to view Ålesund is the low, flat-
topped mountain of Aksla. Steps and a road both lead up to it. I
did once ascend the steep steps on a cold winter's day, but it was a
nerve-racking experience, for a fierce wind was blowing, making
me hang on to the hand-rail, and all the time the dark cloud of a
snowstorm was approaching rapidly across the sea. I reached the
top of those steps as the snowstorm emptied over me like feathers
from a pillow-case. But to be on Aksla on a fine day in any season
of the year is to see Ålesund lying below with an oddly toy-town
look, its buildings clustered on three islands that form the shape of
a giant fish-hook, the water between always busy with boats.

A conveniently sized rock on the pathway makes an excellent
seat on which to rest and take in every aspect of the panoramic
view of the snow-crested Sunnmøre mountains that stretch in the
other direction. Also from Aksla can be seen the sea-islands of
Giske and Vigra, both rich in Viking history. A beautiful girl of
Giske, whose name was Tora, married the Viking King Harald

Hardråde, founder of Oslo, and the sons she bore him, Magnus and Olav Kyrre, both became kings of Norway. Magnus died young, but Olav Kyrre was the strong and just king who founded Bergen. From the island of Vigra came the famous Viking, Gange-Rolv, which means Rolv the Walker, for he was so powerful and heavy that no Nordic horse could carry him. He was a great fighter, but once got so carried away in his lust for battle that he carried out a raid on Norway itself, an action that was indirectly to change history for the laws of the Thing banished him, causing him to seek a base in the Hebrides. From there he attacked France and in 911 founded the duchy of Normandy; from him William the Conqueror was descended.

Ålesund is one of the many ports where the coastal steamers stop long enough for passengers to go ashore, and when north-bound they sail up Romsdal fjord to call at Molde, the Town of the Roses. It lies on the lower south-facing slopes of fir-clad Molde-heia, its trim pastel-coloured buildings reach to the fjord's edge and the six-mile breadth of the island-dotted fjord stretches out before it to the grandeur of 87 mountain peaks rising against the distant sky. From Varden, high above the town, the vista is seen at its best with the Fannefjord sweeping away to the east and the Atlantic gleaming blue, green and grey in the west.

There are flowers everywhere in Molde. Baskets of blossoms hang from the street-lamps, bright gardens surround the neat wooden houses, and roses even grow in profusion on the roof of the town hall. It is the town's sheltered, sun-trapping position, as well as the Gulf Stream lapping its shores, that allows sub-tropical trees and other luxuriant vegetation to grow so far north. In the past Molde was famous for a beautiful crimson rose that was to be found nowhere else in the world. It had a very heavy scent, and it is said that the fragrance was carried far on the breeze, greeting the ships as they came sailing up the fjord.

Then in 1940, during the early days of the German invasion, Molde suffered the fate of all the small towns that sheltered King Håkon and his government in their flight from Oslo. It was bombed until the whole town was ablaze, and today a small monument on the slopes shows where King Håkon and Crown Prince Olav stood watching the destruction, unable to do anything to strike back in defence. When it became possible to assess the damage done it was discovered that the Molde Rose had been completely destroyed. The town was built up again, and other roses planted, but the Molde Rose was sadly missed. Then a few years ago a German horticulturalist stayed in the town while on a touring holiday, and he heard the story of the lost rose. Back in Germany he set about repropagating a rose that would be as near as possible to the original, and the new rose was presented to Molde by the German town of Elmshorn, now linked as a sister town, as a gesture of goodwill and reconciliation. Today the Molde Rose glows crimson in the parks, the gardens and in the flowerbeds that blossom at every corner, but it has very little perfume. That has gone for ever.

Out of the flowers and the well-planned rebuilt town the steepled bell-tower of the new white church rises above the roof-tops. The church was designed in 1957 by the architect Finn Bryn, and the very fine carved altar-piece is entitled 'The Resurrection'; the light from the glass dome above falls full upon it and gives a sky-like luminosity to the blue ceramic walls of the semi-circular chancel. A link with the old church that was bombed is the simple wooden cross hanging on the wall by the chancel steps, its gilt scorched and blackened from that moment when it was snatched from the flames. Above it is suspended a small gilded dove. Stinius Fredriksen and Ornulf Bast are among the leading artists respon-sible for the murals and sculptures that decorate the church, as well as the jewel-bright stained glass of striking design in the north wall. Hanging above the aisle at the west end is the model of an old galleon that hangs by tradition in many of Norway's churches. To a country so linked to the sea it symbolizes the voyage of man from the time he embarks from the womb to face the storms and perils that beset him until finally at the end of his life he reaches the safety of the harbour.

Coming out of the church you are faced with a delightful rose-park with fountains playing and seats on which to rest and gaze out over the great fjord. It is difficult to realize that you are actually on the roof of the town hall! The Oslo architects, Rodahl and Cappelan, designed the building in such a way that the copper and smoked glass frontage with its wide steps and fore-court cannot be seen from the road or from the steps that lead to the church. You are allowed to view the huge lobby of the town hall with its indoor fountain and glass doors that lead to a large concert and lecture hall. Visitors often remark on the size of the building, but Molde is the administrative and business centre for the counties of Møre and Romsdal, although the town's popula-tion numbers a mere 18,500.

Molde hospital is situated on the slopes at a quiet distance from the centre of town, and it was here that my son had his appendix removed, so I had ample opportunity to see at first hand its splendid efficiency. My son knew every surgeon, doctor and nurse by name, as it is the courteous custom of all branches of the medical profession to introduce themselves with a formal hand-shake when speaking to or attending for the first time a patient newly come into the wards.

If taken ill on holiday there is no better place to be than a Nor-wegian hospital, most of which have been rebuilt since World War II and have specialists in attendance with the latest equip-ment for diagnosis and treatment. Moreover, there is a reciprocal arrangement with the British health service, which removes the terrible worry about mounting costs that can hinder recovery in other places abroad. When consulting a doctor about a minor matter he has to be paid on the spot, and a receipt is given. The Norwegian health service does not cover prescribed drugs, except in hospital, and these must be purchased at the centralized *Apoteks* (chemists), which are stark and clinical and sell nothing else as a sideline.

Molde's annual summer Festival of Contemporary Arts includes concerts of both modern and classical music, ballet, poetry read-ings, plays, and a jazz festival that gathers leading artists from both sides of the Atlantic.

The guides in the Romsdal open-air museum at Molde are

usually students making vacation money, and both boys and girls wear national costume. It is a well-signposted walk uphill to the museum from the centre of the town, and about 20 ancient houses from the district are grouped by a lake amid copper-beech, ash, lime, and a host of other trees that grow with such luxuriance in Molde's mild climate. The guides' English is always fluent, but often quaint mis-translations give extra pleasure to the ear. I enjoyed being told by a serious young guide that the old kitchen utensil that I was inspecting was for the roasting of 'coffee-peas' in the 'glows' of the fire. It gave me added pleasure to hear that the wooden containers had held 'bunches' of salt, and in the fourteenth-century Holt cottage that the sleepers in the beds would have kept themselves warm under 'mutton-skins' at night. The church in the museum was used after the destruction of the town until the new church was built, and its bell was rung with such joyful exuberance on Liberation Day that it cracked and broke under the strain !

Molde was once the childhood home of Bjørnstjerne Bjørnson, who went to school there, and was the first to give it the title of Rose Town. Appropriately his statue stands near the college, and on Constitution Day he is adorned with a student's jaunty scarlet cap. Ibsen also lived for a while in Molde, and his paintings of the Romsdal mountains show that he was an artist of the brush as well as the pen.

Fjord ferries give inexpensive rides in all directions from the quay where in 1940 all of Norway's gold was shipped out to England before it could fall into German hands. A fjord-bus leaves every half an hour for the island of Hjertøya with its fine bathing beach, and other islands and bathing beaches are within easy reach. There is a fisheries museum on Hjertøya that is set up like a fishing village, telling the story of the fishermen of the Romsdal coast and of the women who waited for them. There is a 'do-it-yourself' log-kitchen, hung with nets and furnished with wooden tables and barrel seats, where you can cook and eat the fish you have caught yourself either from the shore or in a hired boat on the fjord.

Excursions further afield go to the Holy Island of Veøy with its medieval church that was once visited by pilgrims, and to the picturesque fishing village of Bud and the wind-blown island of Ona where no trees grow. It was from Ona's neighbouring island of Harøy that Inge became one of thousands of young patriots who escaped from their occupied country to join the Free Norwegian Forces in Britain. Ignoring German posters warning that any attempt to leave Norway meant the death penalty, they set off in anything that they could beg, borrow or steal, as long as it would stay afloat. There are a thousand tales told of incidents both humorous and tragic that involved getting possession of a boat. Skippers and fishermen turned a blind eye as their precious means of livelihood went sailing out under the cover of darkness crammed with men intent on taking up arms to free their country from another shore.

One snowy March night in 1941 Inge and 12 friends and fellow apprentices were able to put their escape plans into action. A posted lookout came rushing to tell them that a fishing-boat had unloaded, and was there for the taking. They snatched up what they needed for the journey, and went to break open a German warehouse to roll out the drums of oil that they needed to get them across the North Sea. It was a nerve-racking experience with German soldiers near by, and at the height of it there came a clatter and a splash that made everybody freeze. But it was only one of the youths' toothbrush and mug that he hadn't had time to put in his rucksack, and had set down in the way of one of the rolling drums. Once on board, one youth took the wheel and all the rest crouched down in hiding. Near the sentry turret the engine was switched off and they drifted, fearful that any moment a searchlight would be switched on them, but all went well, and soon they were on the open sea.

But it was a doomed voyage. Although no German plane or patrol vessel spotted them a terrible storm blew up, and when they were within sight of the Shetlands the engine gave out. For seven days and nights they tossed helplessly on the mountainous seas, and finally they were blown back to Norway, coming ashore south of Ålesund. They hung out fishing-nets to look as though they were just another law-abiding boat that had been damaged in the storm. Then they scattered, knowing it was only a matter of time before the Germans identified the boat. Of those 13 youths four were caught and shot. Inge went to his home in Tresfjord, stayed there a week and told his family nothing of his misadventure for their own safety. Then word came secretly that another boat was ready. He got up at five o'clock on the morning of his departure from home only to find that his mother had got up before him to make his breakfast. At the moment of parting, although he tried to behave as though nothing unusual was afoot, his mother took him by the arms. 'Don't let the Germans get you!' she implored frantically. She stood on the porch of the farmhouse to watch him out of sight. Five years were to pass before they met again. During that time he served with the Free Norwegian Air Force, the second escape having gone quite smoothly on a tiny boat called *Fiskegutten* (Fishing Boy) that had come safely to harbour in the Shetlands. He returned home in 1945 to find all the flags in the valley flying for him, and a civic reception to welcome him back again.

Travelling onwards up the coast is to come to Kristiansund where the *klip-fisk* (dried fish), lying like pale leaves, dries hard on the rocks in the wind and sun, and in the large processing factories. The town, like Ålesund, is built on three islands, and its klip-fisk trade dates back to 1691 when Jappe Ippes, a foresighted Dutchman, settled in the town and started the industry, exporting the dried product in vast amounts to Catholic countries where it was eaten on fast days. Kristiansund, another place on the route of the coastal steamers, still holds the position of the major port of the klip-fisk export trade, and ships of all kinds, as well as Norway's largest trawler fleet, keep the water full of seafaring traffic. The town itself, rebuilt after the bombing in 1940, rises up in terraces, and many bridges span the narrow sounds that reflect the passing scene like so many mirrors.

Ferry and road from Kristiansund lead to Sandvika, where larch seedlings brought from Scotland in 1800 have grown to form a

16   Looking towards Andalsnes from the Trollsteg Pass

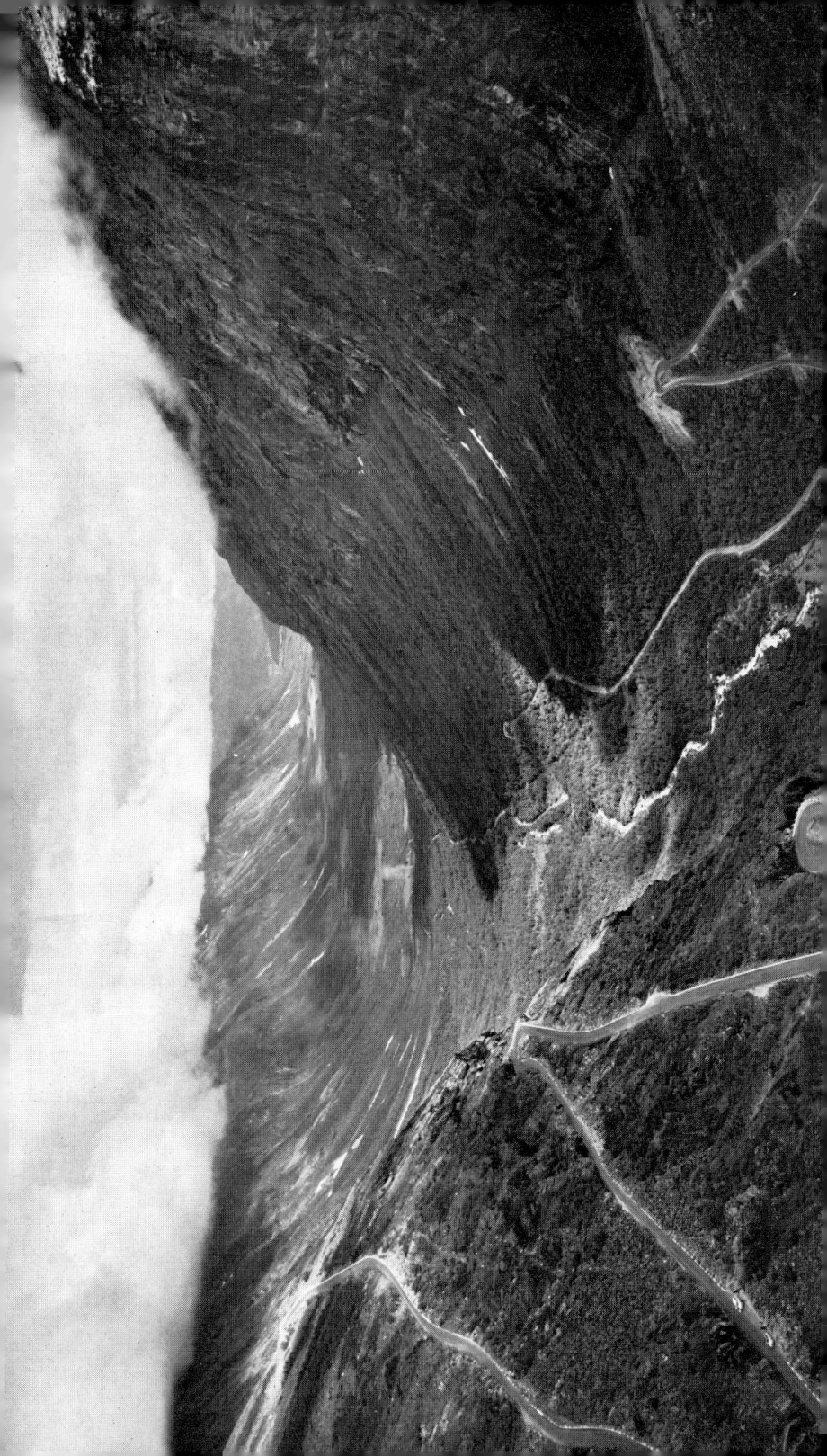

lovely avenue and have spread out over much of the Tingvoll peninsula. Everywhere in the fjord country the soil welcomes the seeds that fall on it, trees, plants, and flowers springing out from any tiny patch of soil lodged on the seemingly bare face of a mountain. Blueberries, wild scarlet cranberries, and the high mountain cloudberry, which looks like an orange blackberry, but has its own delicate and special taste, bring out half the population to pick for the deep-freeze installed in almost every home. So abundant is this harvest of wild berries that some factories that employ a lot of women have special berry-picking holidays – usually the fourth week to which all are entitled in this four weeks' paid holiday country (three are taken at a stretch in the height of summer).

Housewives take a pride in gathering wild flowers for special festive occasions, it being considered a far greater compliment to the guests to have flowers you have gathered yourself on the table than blooms from a florist – the reason why many hotels often use wild blossoms and plants on their tables too. Yet the Norwegians are great givers of professionally arranged bouquets, and as nobody keeps age a secret in Norway floral tributes come in abundance on that first birthday of importance to be celebrated – the day of confirmation being akin to coming of age – that of reaching 40 ! In the country it means open house all day, and – as in the towns – a party in the evening. The presents are extremely lavish for both men and women, a display mounting up to look like an arrangement of wedding gifts, for there is much giving of hand-beaten pewter, silver, and crystal. This happens again at the 50th and 60th birthdays, and at 70 you get your photograph in the local paper. Then on it goes, one women's magazine making a point of sending a birthday cake to all women reaching their 100th birthday.

It is on occasions such as these that Norwegian housewives keep a table laden with food to refresh visitors at whatever hour during the day they choose to drop in, a custom having its roots deep in the past when farmhouses always had a *kolt bord* (cold table) of meats, cheeses, bread and so on ready for anyone that came. The kolt bord that appears at lunchtime in hotels and more expensive

17   The Geiranger Fjord, seen from the Eagle Road

restaurants, which also includes hot food now (you are expected to help yourself as many times as you like from both), originates from this custom, and even now it is impossible to visit farming friends without being expected to stay for a meal, or at the very least to drink coffee and eat from a variety of cakes that the Norwegian housewife always seems to have ready.

The *blöt kaker*, the special cream cakes with their layers of sponge and fruit, could hold pride of place in any *pâtisserie* on the Champs Elysées, but there are also many good things and a host of delicacies to be eaten in Norway. Look out for the crayfish, mountain trout, *rok ørrett* (salted trout), marinated herring, lobster, smoked eel, smoked and fresh salmon, and *gravlaks*, which is salmon cured in brandy and fresh dill, called one of the seven wonders of Scandinavia.

Then there is *spekemat* – preserved meats and sausages made from salted, smoked, and matured reindeer, lamb, mutton, and other meats. Other excellent fare is roast reindeer, reindeer tongue, ptarmigan and other game. Not to be missed is the turbot and also halibut, which often appears reasonably priced on the ordinary day-to-day menus in the excellent small restaurants and cafeterias; the Norwegians can even make cod taste out of this world, serving it with a melted butter sauce and a cool cucumber salad. Much praise by tourists is usually handed out to the Norwegian *smørrebrød*, which is beautiful to look at and most palatable, but soggy versions in other parts of the world have rather spoilt my taste for them; moreover they are very expensive for what they are, and if taking a hungry family in for a quick meal in a cafeteria it is much better to plump for a dish of the day, which will be far more filling and probably cost less. There is always the choice of large or small portions, and it is as well to remember that a large portion really means what it says – probably two or three pork chops, for example – and so a small is usually enough for the average appetite.

One final delicacy that deserves a mention is the small, sweet wild strawberry that grows all over Norway and is there for the taking.

5. Trondheim and District

From the 'Hill of Joy' the pilgrims used to catch their first glimpse of the city of Trondheim. At that time in the Middle Ages it was still known by the old Viking name of Nidaros, which is retained by the cathedral today. The city was founded by the Christian Viking king, Olav Tryggvasson, whose statue stands on a tall column in the centre of the market square where large Norwegian flags flutter between the trees. Trondheim is situated in a triangular peninsula, spilling over the bridges that span the River Nid, which loops to pass the city on two sides before flowing into Trondheimsfjord which flanks the third bank. As Nidaros the city was the capital, and has held a position of importance in the country's history, religion, and culture ever since. Today it is Norway's third largest city, lying some 250 miles south of the Arctic Circle, a blending of sombre Gothic stone, rococo splendour, wooden-frame architecture in palette colours and rows of ancient wharves.

At Stiklestad near Trondheim on 29 July 1030 King Olav Haraldsson, who was destined to become Norway's patron saint, was slain in battle. The kingdom of Norway had been split up again after the death of Olav Tryggvasson, and King Olav Haraldsson, who had made his mark in England by pulling down London Bridge with ropes and strong Viking oarsmen, returned to take up a stormy, war-stricken rein in which he sought to complete Olav Tryggvasson's work in making Norway a wholly Christian country. The old gods were hard to banish. With his religious fervour and his love of beautiful women he is one of the sagas' most powerful personalities, and after a temporary retreat into

Sweden and Russia he marched to Stiklestad to beat his enemies once and for all time. He was slain in the battle and with great sorrowing was buried in a sandy grave by the River Nid. Soon miraculous happenings were reported on the site of his grave, and when it was opened up the king's exhumed body was discovered to be unmarred by a year's burial, and his hair and finger-nails had grown. He was placed in a shrine in the town's little wooden church, and declared to be a saint and a martyr. Further proof of his divinity was forthcoming in the spring with healing powers that suddenly came up out of the place where his body had lain. Through death St Olav achieved what he had failed to do during his lifetime, for the whole of Norway became converted to Christianity as word of what had happened spread.

St Olav's spring is now enclosed in a corner of the ambulatory in Trondheim's beautiful Nidaros cathedral, built on the site of the first stone church raised over the place of the grave in 1070 by King Olav Kyrre. The original stonework and foundations have been pin-pointed through excavation and research. The archbishop's see was established in 1153, and Archbishop Eystein Erlendsson began the replacement of the stone church with a cathedral – a cathedral to take its place with the magnificent Gothic cathedrals being raised all over Europe at that time. To St Olav's holy shrine in Nidaros cathedral came countless thousands of pilgrims from all parts of the Catholic world.

I had to wait quite a while before I could view the cathedral the first time I was in Trondheim. It was a Saturday afternoon, and one wedding after another was taking place. I took a quick glimpse between ceremonies, getting a lightning impression of a rich rose window radiating a shimmering coloured glow, a blend of romanesque, Cistercian and Gothic in sombre grey-green soapstone and the great altar with a huge silver crucifix. Since then I have returned many times to Trondheim and have taken my time wandering round the cathedral, where the English medieval craftsmen who worked on it have left evidence of their presence in styles identifiable with Ely, Lincoln, and Canterbury cathedrals. Seven kings and three queens have been crowned there, the last

being King Håkon vii in 1906. The present King, Olav v, chose to
be blessed in the cathedral after succeeding to the throne in 1957.

Throughout the centuries outbreaks of fire ravaged the cathedral, and in time of war there was plundering by both the Danes
and the Swedes, but since 1869 it has been magnificently restored
and enriched. St Olav lies by the high altar, but nobody today
knows the exact spot, for in 1564 the Swedes stole his silver shrine
and when it was recovered it was placed in an open grave until a
few years later the Danish king ordered it to be covered in. The
battle of Stiklestad and the canonization of St Olav are shown in
stained glass, all the windows being the life's work of Gabriel
Kielland. A sculpture of St Olav in the eastern chapel is by Gustav
Vigeland, who also did the polychrome figures on the choir screen
wall, as well as two angels in the nave's arcade and a number of the
gargoyles. Other sculptural work is by Wilhelm Rasmussen, who
carved the market-square statue of Olav Tryggvasson.

A link with King Håkon's wartime exile is the red ensign hanging in the south transept, which is from the British ship *Norfolk*
that brought him home again to Norway in 1945. The other ensign
hanging there was presented by H.M.S. *Mackay*, the first British
ship to visit Trondheim after the liberation.

At the back of the cathedral and set amid lawns is the 1,000-
year-old archbishop's palace that has witnessed so many troubled
times. Over the entrance to the weighing-house hangs the crest of
the last archbishop of Norway, Archbishop Engelbrigtson, who
fled from the Danes to the Netherlands at the time of the Reforma-
tion in 1537. To the north of the city is his castle, Steinvikholm, in
which he had hoped to withstand a Danish attack, and where he
unpleasantly smoked an enemy to death on Christmas Eve in
1535. In the palace the regalia room is particularly beautiful, the
ceiling and walls covered with paintings of leaves and flowers and
hunting scenes in rich tones that date from the early 1600s. The
reception room, restored a few years ago, was used for the first
time in 1969 when King Olav went to the palace with Queen
Elizabeth ii during her visit to Norway.

When leaving the cathedral precints it is a short walk to see the

old red wooden bridge, strangely oriental in appearance with
something of the pagoda-look of the stave churches, that spans the
river. The ancient, high-gabled warehouses, painted saxe-blue,
green, russet, and yellow, throw a rippled reflection into the tranquil water, which has been used by trading ships since Viking
times. In these warehouses Trondheim herrings have been smoked
and stored throughout the centuries, and the black rotting timbers
of the supports bear witness to the age of the wharves. Twenty-five
of them date back to the seventeenth century, fire having played
havoc with the wooden buildings from time to time, causing them
to be rebuilt again and again since they first stretched a full 300
yards in the mid eleventh century, a length which had doubled a
century later.

The very wide avenues of Trondheim, such as Munk Gate
which runs from the cathedral gates to spear its way through the
market square, are due to the re-planning and rebuilding of the
city after a great fire in 1681 by a Norwegian with French blood
in his veins, Jean Carper de Cicignon. So many wooden houses
erected from that time give grace and charm in tiny bow-fronted
goldsmiths' shops, mansions with wooden lace and delightful
entrances, and the baroque façades of whole streets of houses
nudging each other wall to wall, the lintels carved and picked out
in a variety of colours.

Loveliest of all these buildings is Stiftgården, the royal residence in Trondheim, which was erected in 1774–8 by a rich
widow, Cecilie Christine Schøller, who competed with two rivals
to have the grandest house in the whole of Trondheim. It is a
rococo treasure, one of the largest wooden buildings in Europe,
approached by a double flight of steps with a spun sugar balustrade
ornamented with the royal cipher. Many spacious rooms lead off
the central hall that runs right through the house, so rich in atmosphere that it seems that only minutes have passed since Fru
Schøller left the room with a swirl of pale satin and the flutter of
a fan. It is amazing that the house has escaped the hazard of fire
through the years, and today it is under the constant watch of
Trondheim's fire department.

From a rocky eminence the seventeenth-century fortress of Kristiansten looks out over Trondheim and the island of Munkholmen humped in the fjord. The fortress has withstood many sieges without ever falling to the enemy, and has changed little since Jean Casper de Cicignon built it with the same foresight and style that he used for the rest of the town.

Munkholmen is a motorboat trip away. Once it was a grim place where Vikings used to execute their enemies, but death cries gave way to peaceful chanting when one of Norway's first monasteries was built there, and King Magnus the Blind, who ruled in the twelfth century, became a monk of the Order of Cluny there. No trace remains now of the monastery, but Munkholmen offers a pleasant excursion on a warm summer day, and no shadow of Olav Tryggvasson with an enemy's head impaled on a stake will fall across the grass to darken the day.

There are many other islands that can be visited, for there are hundreds within reach, some inhabited, and others that are leafy havens for picnickers and seabirds. Lying out to sea is one particular island, its population consisting mainly of fishermen and their families, and to its only school in 1970 a young schoolmaster went to take up his first teaching post. As the ferry drew near he saw his seven pupils waiting on the quayside. This was the sum total of school-age children on the island, and they had come to welcome their new teacher. The wide scattering of children makes small and manageable classes the rule rather than the exception, and the standard of education is kept at a commendable level.

One of Trondheim's most famous sons was the sea hero, Peter Wessel, whose childhood was spent at Ringve Manor, which was included in his mother's dowry when she married Alderman Jan Wessel in 1671. Peter Wessel, better known as Tordenskjold (Thunder Shield) was a brilliant officer, resourceful, quick-witted and fearless, whose victories at sea were often achieved against overwhelming odds, as in September 1712, when he completely destroyed the Swedish transport fleet (the great enemy of Norway and Denmark at that time being King Karl XII of Sweden). A delightful tale is told of Tordenskjold's audacity when he ran out

of ammunition while engaged in battle with a Swedish ship com-
manded by an Englishman. Tordenskjold impudently shouted a
request to his opponent for the loan of powder and shot to finish
the fight. The Englishman appreciated the joke, and the two of
them ended up having a glass of wine together. While still young
Tordenskjold was knighted and made an admiral, and when peace
came he left for England to marry a beautiful heiress. In Hannover
a Swedish colonel picked a quarrel with him and challenged him
to a duel: Tordenskjold was killed, but there is no doubt that there
was trickery afoot and it was more a murder than a duel.

Tordenskjold's home at Ringve Manor is reached through a
leafy avenue in an old park. It is a house built in typical Trøndelag
style and most of its interior has been left unchanged since it was
built in 1650. It is grouped with other buildings by a spacious
courtyard, and in the kitchen true Norwegian refreshments can
be had in a quaint old setting.

A unique music museum is also housed at Ringve Manor, the
property having been bequeathed to the nation in 1946 by its
last owner, the Belgian consul in Trondheim, Christian Anker
Bachke. It was his wife, the Russian-born Victoria Rostin, who
fulfilled his dream that the two museums should come into existence. She said of him: 'My husband had three great loves. Now
you will think perhaps that I came first – but no, it was Ringve
Manor. Nor was I his second great love either, it was his music.
His third great love, however, that was me indeed!' Before her
death in 1963 Victoria Bachke created a living museum where
hundreds of instruments, many of them very old and very rare,
can be both seen and heard. Each *salon* is devoted to a particular
period, such as that of Beethoven, Grieg, or Tchaikovsky; the
furniture and décor enhance the instruments on display. The
harpsichord in the Mozart room with its silk panelling and crystal
chandelier is from the Galerie des Glaces at the Palace of
Versailles, for Victoria Bachke went far afield to gather her
splendid collection, and the little grand piano in the same room
was made in 1783 by Johann Andreas Stein and is often played at
concerts given at the manor.

The final room is the nursery, which is full of musical toys of all ages. Among all the horns and trumpets there is the Norwegian *lur*, a long, thin horn made of bark that was used by girls on the saeters in the past to call in the cattle at milking time and takes its place in many old folk tales of magic in the mountains.

Trondheim is not so steeped in the past that it has no time for the present. It has the country's third most important university, and an Advanced Shipping Laboratory that is concerned with the activities of the busy port. Its golf course is the most northerly in the world, and every Midsummer Eve the chance is offered to compete in the Midnight Golf Tournament, which is played from 11 p.m. through to 1–2 a.m. in the bright daylight glow of the non-existent night! First-timers receive a special certificate to show that they have competed in this unique event.

Branching out from Trondheim into its twin counties of North and South Trøndelag there is much to see. The countryside is wild and beautiful with high mountains, deep wooded ravines, rushing rivers where the salmon leap and the opal gleam of lakes. It is not far to Stiklestad to see the battlefield where St Olav died of his wounds in 1030; the church there was raised a hundred years after his death on the place where he fell. The axe that he wielded on that day is incorporated into the state arms which date from the thirteenth century; they have a golden lion with a gold-handled silver axe on a crowned scarlet shield, and the Order of St Olav is the highest decoration that can be awarded. Every year on the anniversary of St Olav's death, 29 July, an historical play re-enacts the dramatic events with a fine swirling of cloaks, clashing of arms, and Viking battle-cries. Another link with Viking times is the site of a Thing meeting-place – where laws were passed and justice done – at Frosta, which is also near Trondheim – and Hell!

Most people like to visit the little village of Hell to send a card with its unusual postmark to their friends, but Hell in Norwegian means 'luck', and has no connection with fire and brimstone. After mailing these cards the reindeer rock-carvings of the Stone Age should be seen, being clearly defined although less realistic than the one at Bøla near Snåsavatnet, also in North Trøndelag, which is a life-size reindeer with a splendid span of antlers, chiselled out with great simplicity and beauty of line.

The most recently discovered carvings are at Leirfall in Hegra, a village on the Stjørdal river, also in North Trøndelag. These carvings date from throughout the whole Bronze Age, and hundreds of figures and complete processions troop across the rock surface, the masked dancers part of an ancient ceremony ensuring the fertility of the land and good harvests. There are ships too, unmistakably dragon-headed, and footprints are depicted, a very common symbol of the presence of some divine being that appears again and again in rock carvings all over the country.

The river of Stjørdal is famous for its salmon, and the Victorian anglers came there as early as 1858. George V was among the many famous anglers who have fished there through the years. Sea trout also abound in this river, which is one of many that with the thousands of lakes make the whole of Norway a fisherman's paradise. Trout, red char, grayling, perch, pike, gwyniad, and fresh water herring are among other fish to be caught. The situation of some lakes in the high mountains means a stiff climb to get there, as in parts of Scotland, but the reward of peace, solitude and a meal of fresh trout sizzling in a frying pan over an open fire is beyond price. There is the story of the Norwegian angler who was so used to having a mile-wide mountain lake to himself that he flew into a rage when he saw another angler appear on the far bank. He stomped down the mountainside, grumbling furiously to himself all the way: 'That lake is getting so crowded that someone might as well put up a hot-dog stand!'

In the Snåsa forests some of the best elk-hunting is to be had – over 8,000 are shot throughout the country during the short season of two weeks from September into October. The dressed weight of a large elk is sometimes over 600 pounds. The plentiful red deer are stalked, but the hunting is very difficult, hounds rarely if ever being used, and not more than 2,000 fall to the gun in the 30-day season. Conditions for hunting are strictly laid down, often a veterinary surgeon must be present at a kill, and all those who own guns, even the landowners on whose territory the game roam, must attend target practice before their licences may be renewed. Everything is done to prevent any unnecessary suffering being caused to a hunted animal. The shooting of ptarmigan or white grouse, which lives in all the mountainous districts, is extremely popular, and other birds shot annually are black grouse, hazel grouse, woodcock, wild geese, ducks, and some seabirds. On the whole wild life in Norway is on the increase, and even the brown bear has reappeared in the mountains at Hønefoss. My father-in-law, who is in his 90s, remembers when the last bear invaded the valley of Øvstedal. He was a very small boy, but joined in with the others in banging saucepans and blowing horns to frighten the bear back over the mountains.

The most famous elk ever to be hunted in Norway has a statue raised to it in Røros in South Trøndelag, which is unlike any other town in Norway. Situated on the great Røros plateau, not far from the Swedish border, Røros has been a mining community since 1644 when the elk, which was being hunted by a local farmer, kicked up clods of earth that held a red-gold gleam. A statue of the farmer, Hans Olsen Åsen, with his mining lamp in his hand, his wife beside him, stands near the old copper foundry with the enormous wooden wheel, the smelting huts and the old bell that rang the shifts.

This richly romantic and carefully preserved town, the river swirling through it, has been immortalized in the famous novels of its past and present by Johan Falkberget, who died in 1967. Whole streets stand unchanged by time, and wood smoke still drifts from the chimneys of the miners' ancient turf-roofed, golden- and black-timbered cottages as it did when they were first built nearly 300 years ago. The cottages are now cheerily and cosily occupied by very present-day Røros folk, who cherish the past as much as they look to the future. Other more elegant houses, painted peach, grey and white, lintels delicately ornamented, which once belonged to the more affluent section of the community are also very much alive, and under the quaint hanging trade-signs of spectacles, a watch, a miner's lamp, a baker's *kringle* (bread roll), to mention a few, both professional and business-men attend to their affairs.

The octagonal church is the only stone building in old Røros. It was erected in 1784, and can seat exactly half the present population. An interesting feature is the crossed mining tools above each of the clock faces in the church tower. The farmstead of the man who first discovered the copper still stands, and a Hans Olsen Åsen of the 11th generation lives in it today. It was feared for a long time that the copper in the vicinity of Røros was coming to an end, but fresh sources on the Røros plateau have revitalized the industry.

In recent years the town has provided the background for several well-known films, and has earned itself the title of the Hollywood of Norway. In winter it is particularly spectacular, and the plateau offers the most wonderful skiing, making it necessary to book a hotel at Røros a year ahead. In summer there are excellent marked walks for ramblers, who can plan a route to link up with the chalets run by the Norwegian Touring Club which are to be found all over Norway.

6. North Norway

Travelling northwards on the E.6 over the great Salt mountain you see the road suddenly curve away in the distance towards a solitary low, wooden building, its yellow paintwork making a speck of colour in the bleak landscape. The flags of many nations flutter over the windows, and a thick cluster of parked cars shows that this is a halting place of some importance. White boulders stretch away in a thin line to the east and west of the road. It is the Arctic Circle.

It is definitely more interesting to cross the Arctic Circle by sea or road than by the train, which merely gives a long whistle and does not stop. At sea Father Neptune suddenly appears on board the coastal steamers in the tourist season, and at the roadside stands a large meridian stone cut with runic-style letters stating 'Polar Cirkel', which everybody is photographing. I have crossed the 'Polar Cirkel' in blistering sunshine, fog, rain, and in a wind so cold that it seemed dangerous to breathe in it. In the yellow building the souvenir shop does a roaring trade in postcards that are franked with the Arctic Circle's own postmark, and certificates, signed by a witness, can be bought as further proof that Jack Frost's domain has been entered, and on whose authority the certificates are issued, according to the information on them!

While having a snack or a cup of coffee the warning about reindeer herds can be duly read and taken in, for the regions of the wild reindeer have been left far behind, and the territory has been reached where the herds are domesticated and owned by one of the most fascinating of all nomadic peoples, the Lapps. The displayed notice sums it all up: 'You are now in a reindeer herding district. Reindeer herding is an industry from prehistoric times in this part of the country and reserved for the Lapps, a privilege established by law. The taming of reindeer is beset with difficulties, and the Lapps would appreciate it if you would cooperate. Do not approach grazing reindeer. You may frighten the females away from the calves and scatter the flock. Ask permission if you wish to approach a reindeer fence when work among reindeer is going on. Keep away and do not approach a flock being driven by. Drivers, do not increase speed after a reindeer on the road – it will become reluctant to leave the road, and on the point of exhaustion may turn on the car. At night lower the lights and drive with care.'

On sunny days in these mountains the Svartisen glacier shines a deep indigo blue, but on dull days it truly deserves the name of 'black ice'. It has been there since the Ice Age and covers an area of 200 square miles, making it the second largest glacier in Norway. But being north of the Arctic Circle does not mean you have entered a chill region of ice and snow and barren rock. Passing from the high mountains down to sea-level again is to come upon lush green valleys, wooded slopes, and well-tended farms. Habitation between towns becomes sparser, and often garages warn that long distances lie ahead and they offer the last chance to buy petrol for 50 miles or more.

The railway ends at Bodø, the last stretch being the Nordland Line that covers the 453 miles from Trondheim. Being within easy reach of many interesting places Bodø has become a growing tourist centre. The midnight sun is visible here from 5 June to 9 July, and with night completely banished there seems to be twice as much time available in which to do everything. A sleeping mask for the eyes is a useful item, for Norwegians favour filmy curtains and a sun-filled room is not inducive to sleep when physical tiredness can no longer be kept at bay. North Norwegians seem to abandon sleep in summertime. Looking out of the window in any of the small hours is to see people strolling in the sun, on their way for a swim or chatting on the street corner. Summer is a blissful, halcyon time, and they do not waste a moment of it.

Bodø is a neatly spaced town, the capital of Nordland, green with trees. A statue of King Håkon in army uniform stands by the market place, a link with those days in 1940 when North Norway still held out against the Germans. The town is backed by great mountains, and in particular Mount Rønvikfjell gives a spectacular view towards islands far out at sea, the most important being those of the Lofoten archipelago. A few miles away from the town is the famous *Saltstraum* where four times a day a seething maelstrom is formed when tidal currents force the water through the narrow neck of the fjord. There is a terrifying violence to that great surging of tortured water, the shining green folding in upon itself, flecked with foam, hissing and bubbling, killing all the fish caught up in it. Local people often pick up salmon, cod, and halibut that have been victims of the maelstrom, but it is also a popular place for catching coalfish, one after another being swung gleaming out of the water by the anglers that go there. In the autumn barrels are quickly filled and find a ready market.

Excursions can be made to the Lofoten islands from Bodø by steamship and seaplane. From the air they rise like the great fangs of some sea-monster hidden below the surface of the water, a sight in winter of almost eerie beauty that brings the old Norse legends very much alive, but to approach by sea is almost as dramatic, for you are met by the torn peaks and deep-set glaciers of the Lofoten Wall that stretches a full 60 miles. Perhaps it was in waters such as these that the god Tor went fishing for the sea-serpent, using the head of an ox as bait, and when the serpent took it Tor pulled so hard on the line that his feet went right through the bottom of the boat to rest on the sea-bed. Unfortunately the oarsman in the boat took fright and cut the line, so that the serpent got away. That was Tor's account anyway. Surely the fishing tale to end all fishing tales!

It is said that more artists and businessmen live on the Lofoten Islands than fishermen, who come from far away to join the fleets that gather there. Svolvær, which dates back to the Middle Ages, is the chief town, but is no more than a village in size with a boxy white church standing on a rise; its modern buildings and well-kept wooden houses in paintbox hues, windows full of flowering plants, lie clustered like rings on fingers of land that stretch out into the sea. Above the village towers the Svolvær goat, a mountain that has two horns, and it is a local speciality of experienced climbers to leap the five feet between them.

Svolvær, with its aroma of salt and flowers, fish-heads and ship engine-oil, is the administrative centre of the fisheries. It is a busy hub, particularly in the season when thousands of fishing smacks jam-pack the harbour, making it as full of masts as spikes on a hedgehog, as they gather there in readiness to harvest the rich fishing grounds on the shallow coastal banks near by.

Triangular racks of drying cod, which have been gutted and cleaned, stand in the open air, a feature of Svolvær as well as of most of the fishing-ports in north Norway where the cold, bacteria-free air is perfect for producing stockfish. To walk beneath an archway of these racks is like being in the pale-gold nave of a cathedral, the sun sprinkling through to pattern the ground. This way of drying cod has not changed since Viking times, when the paper-dry product was stowed aboard the longships as part of the rations for a voyage. One kilo of stockfish has the same nutritional value as five of fresh fish – not that the Vikings would have been aware of that.

For those who have time to linger, or who have rented one of the fishermen's cottages, the Lofotens have many sights of interest. There is the island of Røst where there are more seabirds than there are people in the whole of Norway, and Mount Vågekallen where a strange twist in the rock has formed the shape of a fisherman carrying a spar, to which by tradition every youth joining the Lofoten fisheries for the first time bows deeply and doffs his hat. Among the small coastal villages tucked away under the mountains is Stamsund, which owes its existence to one man, Julius M. Johansen, who created a site for it out of the rock there in the early 1900s. Kabelvåg is the oldest village of all, for boat-shelters were built there as long ago as 1120 with development into a trade centre following soon afterwards.

18 *Nidaros Cathedral, Trondheim*

19 *Romanesque arch, north transept, Nidaros Cathedral*

20   *A farm by Loen Lake, Nordfjord*

Ugly seas and heavy storms still bring danger to the life of the present-day Lofoten fisherman, but nothing to compare with the past when the fishing-smacks set out with only sail and skill to bring them safely home again. Major Ingvar Stamnes of the Royal Norwegian Air Force showed me a collection of tools, nets and equipment from the old Lofoten fishing days that had been in his family for many years. Nothing could have conjured up the rigours of those hard times at sea better than the simply-made gadget that looked like a large cork-screw, which was turned round and round in a block of wood as a form of exercise in the Arctic temperatures to keep hands from freezing and some warmth in the body. The yards of fishing-net were as fine as lace, but extremely strong, hand-made from home-grown flax, and the floats were curls of birch-bark. Major Stamnes gave me a length of fishing-net to keep as a souvenir of the Lofoten Islands, pointing out that the birch-bark floats had preceded cork and green glass. 'Now the floats are made of orange *plastic*!' he said with a sigh.

Back on the mainland Narvik welcomes visitors with its crest of a gold anchor on a scarlet background. It lies on a peninsula between two small fjords, facing the inner Ofot fjord, seemingly held within a diadem of peaks. The open-air concert hall proclaims the reliability of its summers. The Ofot railway line, to which the town owes its existence, runs right from the harbour to the Swedish border. Although only 26 miles long the line transports annually about half the total quantity of all goods carried by the Norwegian state railways; it was built in four years, being completed in 1902, for the purpose of moving iron ore from the mines in Swedish Lapland to the sea. A statue of one of the workers who built the line stands in Gulbransons Park, a wide-brimmed hat on his head, sledge-hammer in his hand. Tales of the hard slogging that went into the laying-down of the line have become absorbed into the country's folklore; it was an engineering feat, a conquering of heights that set the line through tunnels and cuttings, the way blasted by men who clung like ants to the mountain face. There was a well-known character who cooked for the working gangs: she was a handsome woman with hair black as pitch, which caused her to be known as the 'Black Bear', and the fame of her beauty and her cooking linger on today.

It was Narvik's industrial importance that made the German forces occupy the town strongly on that first day of invasion on 9 April 1940. The Mayor of Narvik at that time, Theodor Broch, described in his book *The Mountains Wait,* now a classic of those times, the astonishment of being awakened by gun-fire and an explosion in the fjord that fateful morning and then going outside to find German troops armed with machine-guns on the bridge, and swastikas flying in the market-place and on the telegraph building. From that moment Narvik leapt into world headlines. To this day most people seem to associate Narvik with the bitter fighting of counter-attack and recapture that took place there.

So firmly did the Germans finally entrench themselves that to this day old fortifications remain, scored deep into rock, the entrance overhung with grass and flowering plants, half-hidden from sight along the pretty winding lanes that lead to the water's edge. The flat stones lapped by the fjord are ideal for picnics, particularly in the evenings when not a breath of wind stirs the fir trees, and the Arctic sunsets turn the sky and sea rose and amber and gold.

The coastal areas in the Arctic are comparatively free of the mosquitoes that plague the inland regions in summertime. Public buildings and private homes have protective netting over windows, but campers and caravanners often have trouble if they have not gone prepared. The mosquitoes, as well as the inedible dryness of the reindeer moss in the summer months, are behind the great migration of Lapps and their herds to the coast every spring. The moss, which appears almost fossilized in the summer, makes a crisp, bloomy carpet that often stretches as far as the eye can see. Until the end of June the far orth is mosquito-free, but inland in July and August watch out!

The capital of Troms county is Tromsø, situated on the beautiful island of Tromsøya, a bird and animal sanctuary where no shooting is allowed at any time of the year. It lies like a great green jewel in the water, thickly speckled on the east with the multi-coloured buildings of the town, and approached by the longest bridge in northern Europe. Facing the bridge and Tromsø Sound is the Tromsdalen Church, known as the Cathedral of the Arctic, consecrated in 1966 and renowned for the unique glass-laid triangular walls and for the incorporation of the surrounding mountains into its design. The peaks soar, held in the clear glass above the altar, a living, ever-changing panorama. In winter time the church shines like a wedge of light, throwing a glow far across the snow.

When I first crossed the three-quarters-of-a-mile long bridge into Tromsø there was a toll of nine kroner for the car, but that was stopped as soon as the bridge was paid for – in a remarkably quick time. It is a system that covers the many lengthy new bridges and tunnels that have shortened so many routes; the *bom-penger* men in their toll-booths vanish as soon as the cost has been recovered.

Tromsø is one of the few towns in the Arctic that escaped destruction in 1944 when the Germans, retreating before the advancing Russians, set fire to everything. Yet Tromsø has suffered from other fires at different times, but the old salty atmosphere of its early eighteenth-century beginnings lingers on. Since it became a shipping and Arctic trading centre at that time, generations of whalers, sealers, and trappers have carried on their business there. The whaling station is still in use, and twice a week whirling clouds of screeching seagulls accompany the arrival of whales that are winched up the slopes. At times the aroma of whaling oil hangs over the town, unnoticed by the residents but offensive to those unused to it. Coal from Spitzbergen mines arrives to be stored and transhipped, and the first sealing ships were fitted out there. The fur trade flourishes, and every third blue fox skin in the world – a particular colour variation of the Arctic fox, the fur of the animal staying blue-grey throughout the year instead of turning white in winter – comes from Norway. Polar bears are now protected to a certain extent, but there was a time when the skins arrived in their hundreds from the far Arctic regions beyond

Norway. Today the only polar bear to be seen in Tromsø is a stuffed one outside a fur-shop in the main street. Its fur has to be replaced every third year as it gets worn out by tourists, adults and children alike, sitting on it to be photographed!

Many Arctic expedition ships have sailed from Tromsø, and a statue of Roald Amundsen stands on the quayside, the hood of his weatherproof jerkin thrown back, his gaze set on the horizon where once there sailed northwards his ships *Gjøa* and *Maud*. Amundsen's last venture was the ill-fated aeroplane flight from Tromsø in 1928, when he set off to search for the Italian explorer Nobile and failed to return. It was from Tromsø's quayside that King Håkon, Crown Prince Olav, and the government left Norway in 1940 for an exile in England that was to last five years. Behind Amundsen's statue looms the spire of the cathedral; this is the most northerly see in Norway. It is a very simple wooden structure, contrasting sharply with the magnificence of Trondheim's cathedral. The walls are painted pale grey and apricot, its pulpit is ornamented with gilt, and it stands among flowerbeds where in July tulips blaze scarlet and orange and yellow, summer flowers in this northern clime.

Tucked away in a corner of Tromsøya island, facing the fjord and other islands beyond, is the unique residence of a Tromsø man, Oivind Dahl, and his wife, Ruth, who own the only private zoo in the Arctic. The house was specially designed by the architect Harry Gangvik to blend into the nature that encloses it and the wild life that can be seen from the windows. Locally it is known as 'Little Paradise', for it has long been a haven for injured wild animals and birds that are treated by Oivind Dahl, healed and then set free again if able to fend for themselves once more; otherwise they remain at the 'Little Paradise', undisturbed, seeing few visitors, leading as natural a life as possible in their captivity. Some of them can be glimpsed through a wall of glass in the south end of the long living-room, the wired enclosures stretching like an airy, transparent wing to the house, shaded by green foliage, bright with the gleam of individual pools.

There was a young seal which for several months occupied the

enclosure next to the wall of glass, and every time it spotted movement in the living-room would hoist itself out of the water to bark
and gain attention. Sometimes it dozed on its back in the sun, its
long-lashed eyes closed in contentment, flippers languid. It had
been rescued by the skipper of a cod-fishing trawler from an ice-
flow drifting in the Arctic Ocean, a baby of less than three weeks,
still in its soft white natal fur, lying beside its dead mother. When
the trawler put in at Tromsø the skipper handed the seal into the
care of Oivind Dahl.

Next to the seal's enclosure is an otter's pool with a choice of
holts into which the graceful, limpid, seemingly boneless creature
darts to eat the large fish tossed to it at feeding time. It loves to
have the full force of the cleaning hose turned on it, and will stand
up, head tilted, eyes shut as though under a waterfall.

Among the birds in the aviary is a Dutch racing pigeon that had
fallen in exhaustion, damaging its wing, on the deck of a Norwegian ship sailing to Bear Island, and when the ship docked at
Tromsø the pigeon was received at 'Little Paradise'. Oivind Dahl
contacted the Dutch owner with the information that the bird was
safe, but its racing days were over. Then he complied with a
request from the Dutchman to give the bird a home.

Other permanent residents are two red foxes, rare enough in the
Arctic, both crippled but specially privileged, for they alone are
allowed into the house. After dinner in the evenings the foxes enter
a tunnel and scratch with their claws on the door of a porthole set
low near the floor of the living-room. When Oivind opens it they
enter to take a tit-bit from his fingers, sometimes to return again
as quickly as they came, and on other occasions to stay for
a while, ignoring and ignored in turn by the dogs in the room.
Guests are often afraid of having their ankles nipped, but Oivind
assures them that this will not happen. Nevertheless they find
it hard to relax when a bright-eyed fox decides to sit under their
chair!

Another feature of this unusual home is the indoor pool set in
the floor of the living-room, fed with crystal clear spring water
through an underground channel from a pond outside. Not for

Oivind Dahl the tranquil flicker of goldfish: in and out of this pool swam rainbow trout when he was breeding them in a plan to restock natural lakes and waterways.

Feeding all the inhabitants of 'Little Paradise' never presents any problems to this man, who even as a small boy brought home all stray and sick animals that needed care. Fish forms the greater part of most of the diets and he catches all that is needed from his own boat, the waters around the island of Tromsøya abounding with so much fish that it is possible to average a bite a minute. His return from one of these fishing trips on a summer night is a scene of white and gold: it is as bright as midday, and the little beaches, made up of white coral and millions of pearly shells, are touched by the glow of the Midnight Sun, ribbing with gold the amber sky that melts into the curious cloudless whiteness of Arctic summer nights. When the returning boat draws near, black against the liquid gold of the fjord, the Dahls' many dogs set up a noisy welcome. But no greeting can surpass the final exotic touch given to the scene by the two enormous, snowy-haired huskies, their long, wolf-like yowls rising in anticipation of a piece of newly-caught fish.

Oivind and Ruth have seen many New Years in alone with their team of huskies on the white tundra, and often – scorning the car – Ruth has travelled with husky and sledge into town to do her shopping at the supermarket, declaring that there is no better way to travel. And surely no more picturesque way either!

Oivind is always on the look-out for wild creatures in distress during the winter months, and one day, returning home on skis in a sudden blizzard, he glimpsed a spot of colour in the snow and thought it was a fox. Quickly he sped towards it, and found a snow-buried child. It had been her scarlet woollen cap that he had sighted. She had alighted from the school bus and lost all sense of direction in an unexpected snowstorm that had blown up to engulf her. Had Oivind not been keeping his customary look-out the child would have died.

Children are picked up by the school bus in darkness and return home again in the same pitch blackness. When they make their own way anywhere in the darkness they have a luminous tab that they flick out of their pockets to catch the light of passing vehicles. Yet daylight does come to the Arctic, even in the heart of winter, illuminating Tromsø with a grey glow for two hours at midday. One great advantage of wintering in the Arctic is that nobody ever catches the common cold!

Oivind and Ruth Dahl are among North Norwegians I have met who would not live anywhere else in the world. The peace of the North and its wild, almost ferocious beauty casts such a spell that even those from more southern areas settle down contentedly and do not find the winters too dark, pointing out that the snow gives off its own glittering radiance, and the Northern Lights are ever on the move across the sky. At the Observatory for Northern Lights in Tromsø I was shown the apparatus that records the activity of the aurora, which is sometimes so strong in winter that radio is cut out. Even in summer it is still studied, although not visible, with the aid of radar techniques and various electrical measurements. I commented on the vast, ankle-length fur coats that were put on for reading outdoor instruments in the depth of winter. 'It gets pretty bleak sometimes,' was the casual understatement of a reply.

The Arctic can also reach sweltering heat in summer, often with temperatures to rival those of the Mediterranean, as was shown to me in the records when I visited the Vervarslinga for Nord-Norge, the meteorological station of North Norway. The entrance hall is enhanced by a magnificent mosaic mural by Marit Bockeue, depicting the sun and every mood of weather. I was taken round by a meteorologist, who was himself a Tønsberg man, but so captivated by the North that he could not think of returning south again. 'So little sleep is needed in the summer,' he said. 'Visitors often call with small children at our house at two o'clock in the morning when we are sitting enjoying the sunshine in the garden. It is a very pleasant way to live.' On the roof of the Vervarslinga that day the temperature was 35°C, and there was a view of crystal-sharp mountains under a cloudless sky the colour of speedwell.

The meteorological station first came into existence in 1866, only three years after the first weather reporting was started by the Paris Observatory. From it are relayed all the reports from the stations that lie even farther north, such as those in Greenland and Svalbard, the name given to the Spitzbergen archipelago that comprises a group of six large and several small islands in the Arctic Ocean, an area of 24,294 square miles, where so much of the stormy weather brews up. In a hundred years the Vervarslinga has had only three directors, the first two holding office for 40 years each, and the third being still in command, a fine example of the longevity of the average Norseman.

The way to round off a visit to Tromsø is to take the cable-car up to Storsteinen for a last view of the island, and perhaps a glimpse of the coastal steamer calling in to give its passengers time to go ashore. Some filming was going on when I was last on Storsteinen. Some Lapps were 'yoiking' in turn for the benefit of a Norwegian film company, each *yoike* being a kind of song peculiar to the man who sings it. The origin of 'yoiking' lies deep in the past, in legends and magic, and a Lapp 'yoikes' of his reindeer, the mountains, a journey, or anything else that makes the song his own personal experience, so that other Lapps associate it only with him, his appearance or some characteristic that he has.

Although a few Lapps are to be seen in the streets of Tromsø and at tourist stations along the roadside, it is farther north at Alta, the village centre of inner Finnmark, that the first step is taken into the heart of the Lapp world. The Norwegian Lapps, who number about 20,000, can be divided into three main groups: the Mountain Lapps, who concentrate on breeding reindeer; the River Lapps, who inhabit inland areas around rivers and lakes, depending on fishing, particularly salmon, as their main source of income, supplemented by some agriculture; finally those who have settled near the coast, known as Sea Lapps, who make a livelihood from agriculture and fishing. This last group has integrated more with the Norwegian people than the others, both through inter-marriage and by branching out through higher education into other work and professional careers.

These sturdy, independent people consider themselves Lapps

first and foremost; their Norwegian citizenship is secondary to them, although all rights are theirs. They speak their own language among themselves and cling to their own customs. They are a short, stockily-built, agile people; the men have wonderfully weather-beaten faces the moment that first youth has passed, and all walk with the characteristic bent-kneed lope that comes from a life spent on skis. Both men and boys wear the same blue-skirted tunics decorated with bands of ornamented scarlet braid, caught in by a wide belt hung with a sheath-knife, blue trousers with high boots and a triangular-peaked blue hat, almost like that of a jester, also trimmed with braid. The Lapp women wear the same blue, the skirts very full and longer on the older women than on the girls, who wear them at knee level. Their bonnets are scarlet, hugging the face, with soft pouchy crowns, and they wear a lot of gold jewellery, the whole outfit completed by a silk shawl, often of a plaid pattern, about the shoulders. Small children are dressed in exact replicas in miniature of the clothes worn by adults. It is certainly an interesting sight to see these picturesquely clad people pushing wire prams around the supermarket in Alta as they buy their supplies.

The Alta supermarket is one of a good selection of shops grouped by a wide street with ample room for parking. One of the most pleasant aspects of motoring in Norway is that there is always plenty of parking space. The road surfaces throughout the country are as variable as the scenery, and although constantly under repair or reconstruction those in the far north are rough and subject to pot-holes, particularly after a spell of rain or bad weather. It is no wonder that many holiday travellers returning from the Arctic write – with the pride of achievement – in the dust coating their vehicles the words: North Cape! Antlers ornamenting the luggage rack are another first-class feature of trips to the Arctic. These can be purchased in the souvenir shops, or from the Lapps themselves, who display goods for sale on racks made of natural birch branches that blend harmoniously with their colourful encampments of wigwam-like tents. There is always a wide choice of reindeer skins, which are amazingly soft, the greys,

25 *Fish being dried, Lofoten Islands*
26 *Svolvaer, Lofotens*

browns and the white all holding a kind of shimmering bloom as they hang there for the purchasing.

From Alta several roads lead across the tundra of the Finnmark plateau to two of the best-known Lapp towns, Kautokeino and Karasjok. Kautokeino is the centre of the largest reindeer district in Norway, a rural region of 4,000 square miles, and until 1600 it was only a winter site for the Lapps. After that it began to develop, being on the way to Finland; the Lapp name for the town is 'Guovdagaeino', which means 'half-way house'. The first church to be built there in 1703 was destroyed by the Germans along with the rest of the town in 1944, but on the same site now stands the wooden, onion-steepled church that is approached by a road cut through the hill that bears another illustrative Lapp name meaning 'tent mound'. The Lapp language is full of rich and descriptive words, and a whole vocabulary for herding reindeer exists, which allows for every characteristic of an animal, every turn of speed, degree of tameness, and so forth, which could not be fully translated into another language. Great pains are taken by Norwegian governments to see that the Lapp heritage is preserved, and special grants encourage the learning of Lappish by teachers, as well as the printing of literature in the language.

School books are in Lappish, and Lapp children far out in the tundra are either picked up by special snowbuses or attend mobile schools. In the past only the unique structure of their nomadic way of life, to which they have clung tenaciously, and their social environment have kept the Lapps from establishing an intellectual cultural tradition. All that is changing, due to the increased opportunities available as well as easier communications, and those Lapps who have already made their mark in the world of art and literature are merely the spearhead of all those that will follow.

No visit to Kautokeino is complete without a visit to the Lapp silversmiths. Among the locally made jewellery in traditional designs is the 'mother's ring', which can be plain or ornate, but has attached to it tiny decorative hoops, each representing a child, so that the number varies according to the size of the wearer's family.

A Lapp woman with many children will proudly display a ring a-shimmer with hoops.

There is always a dazzling display of gold ornamentation at Lapp weddings, which must be among the most colourful in the world. Adding extra brilliance to the Sunday-best costumes in the same scarlet and blue as everyday wear are the multi-coloured streamers that the men attach to their hats. The only touches of white are in the scarf that the bridegroom fastens with a gold brooch on his chest and in the veil of the bride, which is attached to her scarlet bonnet tied with a white bow for the occasion under her chin. As many as ten magnificent gold brooches, some almost as large as a saucer, will keep her silken shawl in place.

Over 200 Lapps leave Kautokeino every spring on 20 April to follow their great herds, at least 50,000 head of reindeer, to the coast. They always travel at night when the snow is crisp and hard, the women and children riding in sledges. Hundreds of miles are covered, and the calves are born on the way. In September slaughtering takes place, for this is the time when the reindeer are at their fattest after the rich grazing at the coast. Then in late September and early October the homeward trek begins, a time when the herdsmen must be on the alert every moment, for it is now that the stags fight each other for the does, and vanquished stags will often break away, taking others with them, unless checked. The Kautokeino Lapps reach home and their winter quarters in time for Christmas.

Karasjok is similar to Kautokeino; the houses are widely spaced, almost scattered in comparison with small townships in other counties, and beyond stretches the tundra, with its forests, rivers, and lakes as far as the eye can see. The Lapp High School at Karasjok offers a permanent exhibition of Lapp handicrafts, a fine selection of the exquisite pewter-thread embroideries, decorated spoons, knife-sheaths, belts, silverware, and many other objects of a high artistic standard. Also in Karasjok is the only museum in Norway devoted entirely to Lapp culture.

Gold is to be found thinly and widely distributed all over Finn-mark, and 37 miles away from Karasjok at Storfossen is a gold-mining camp. It takes about two hours to get there by boat on the Karasjokka River, travelling in one of the long, narrow, flat-bottomed craft that are a traditional feature of this vast area. Originally poles and oars were used to send the boats skimming along, but now the outboard motor speeds up the journey on this swirling, sometimes choppy river. At the camp visitors can stay under canvas and pan for gold – instruction is given and equipment is supplied. The chance of making a fortune is remote, but enough gold has been panned in a week-end to make a wedding ring.

Turning back towards the coast again, across moorland pale with the reindeer moss that feeds the great herds in winter, each animal scraping away the snow to find the juicy plant beneath, you regain the Arctic Highway. There a detour must be made to reach Hammerfest, the most northerly town in the world, but it is worth the hazards of the pitted road through wild and grim-faced countryside that at times seems as barren and deserted as the surface of the moon. Those sailing northwards on the coastal steamers approach the town with grace, sailing into a bay surrounded by rugged mountains that make a natural, weather-protected harbour. Hammerfest has been entirely rebuilt since its destruction in 1944; in the town hall is the club known as the Royal and Ancient Society of Polar Bears that can be visited, and a fine museum devoted to the history of Arctic trapping.

Most of the inhabitants of Hammerfest are employed in the fishing industry – the town has the largest deep-freeze installation in Scandinavia – which is responsible for the town's being listed as one of the 25 most prosperous places to live in on Norwegian soil. It was the first town in Europe to get electric light, due to the foresight of one of its councillors who in 1890 went to the Paris exhibition and saw a revolutionary machine designed for producing electricity. 'Nobody needs that more than we do!' he exclaimed. Everybody else seems to have shared his opinion, for the Hammerfest councillor was the only purchaser of that machine out of the thousands of people who attended the exhibition. In 1891 Hammerfest had the first water-driven power station in Europe, and the following year the streets of the town were lit by electric light. It is easy to imagine the boon it must have been in a winter night that lasts from 21 November to 23 January. Today in Hammerfest, as in all these northern towns, indoor sports arenas, playing fields, and swimming baths give ample opportunity for football and all kinds of competitive sports to be carried on all through the winter, whatever the weather outside.

The last stretch to North Cape lies ahead as Hammerfest is left behind. On the long, lonely route often the single figure of a brightly-clad Lapp, looking a little like a cut-out felt toy against the sombre grey-greens of the landscape, stands at the roadside, waiting for the bus. At first sight there seems to be no sign of habitation, but on drawing nearer an encampment can usually be glimpsed far away in the distance. The Lapps do not attempt to hitch a ride. They are never in a hurry, but take life at a comfortable pace. There is the classic tale of the traveller whose car broke down on a lonely part of the tundra. He made his way to a Lapp encampment, and asked to be conveyed by river boat to his destination. 'With pleasure', answered the Lapps, 'but first you must have a meal with us.' The traveller accepted their hospitality, and when it was over he made it clear as politely as he could that he was anxious to be on his way. 'Not without some good coffee to warm you,' was the reply. He fumed with impatience, gulped his coffee, and then leapt to his feet. 'Now let's go !' But still the Lapps delayed, looking at him with mild surprise. 'We must have a little drink and a smoke.' The traveller thought of all the appointments he was missing, and the hours already lost. 'I'm in a frantic hurry !' he burst out.

The Lapps looked at each other, and then at him. 'Then you should have broken down in your car yesterday,' they said.

Seeing the midnight sun at North Cape is the aim of all those who journey by road, sea, and air to the top of Europe, but it can be something of a gamble. Should the weather change and cloud descend all chance is gone. I remember rain swooping down in July in a totally unexpected drop in the temperature when I had got as far as Honningsvåg on the final stretch across the bleak

Magerøy island to where the 1,000-feet granite cliffs rise pre-
cipitously from the sea, the plateau like a great prow jutting into
the Arctic Ocean. But few people are as unfortunate as the
American who made 12 visits to the North Cape before his
patience was finally rewarded.

The North Cape owes its name to an English explorer, Richard
Chancellor, who sailed these waters in 1553 while searching for
the north-east passage to China. It is a bleak spot even in summer,
but how much worse in winter when waves over 30 feet high lash
against the cliffs. While waiting for the magic hour of midnight on
any day from 14 May to 30 July the North Cape Hall with its
panoramic windows offers the opportunity to take a meal, buy a
North Cape certificate, and get postcards and letters written and
then franked with the North Cape's own postmark.

An extraordinary excitement hangs in the air as everyone starts
glancing at watches, and turns attention on the great blazing ball
that has been sinking towards the horizon, setting sky and sea afire
with its glow. The climactic hour comes, the whole disc of the
midnight sun hangs above the glittering water and then slowly
starts to rise again.

To most people Kirkenes is somewhat of an anticlimax after
the North Cape, but the coastal steamers turn around there for the
voyage back to Bergen. For those who are interested there are
carefully supervised excursions to view the Norwegian–Soviet
border, for this is the only municipality in Norway that lies
shoulder to shoulder with Russia. Kirkenes is a busy port, millions
of tons of iron ore being mined annually in the region, and there
is a vigorous bustle in the atmosphere of this town that lies like
neatly arranged nursery building bricks in a host of primary
colours, backed by rugged hills where the orange cloudberries grow
in profusion.

In recent years Norway, Sweden and Finland have combined
in a joint effort to promote their Arctic regions as a tourist centre
to compete with all others in the world as offering holidays with a
difference in summer, and unsurpassed skiing in the snowy
months. Truly they can boast of being able to ensure more summer

sun than any other inhabited area, as well as pure air, unpolluted rivers, lakes, and sea, and magnificent scenery enhanced by the abundance of wild flowers that grow in a shimmering carpet. In addition there are those most elusive of all commodities – peace, stillness and uncrowded space in which to wander at will. The brown bear inhabits these regions, also the wolf, but the chances of seeing them are very remote, for the struggle for survival has made them shy away from man. Naturally the Arctic is no place for those who want night life on their summer holidays, but then that is of no importance to those who become enchanted with the Arctic. After all, there are no nights.

Turning southwards, those who travel by sea will call at several ports again before leaving Arctic waters, and sail past islands where thousands of kittywakes nest and ospreys are to be seen; those travelling by air will save many hours of retracing tracks already covered. By road there are no short cuts, but for those like myself this is no hardship, and the antlers on passing cars shine like gleaming trophies as eventually the Arctic Circle is crossed and left behind.

7. Central Mountains and Eastern Valleys

Returning from the North across the Dovre mountains by car it was certainly a surprise to meet a traffic block. Admittedly it was the height of the tourist season in July, but it was obvious that something very out of the ordinary must have happened. It did not take long to discover the reason. A great musk-ox, a bull standing a full five feet at the shoulders and weighing about 800 pounds, had taken it into his head to pause for a while in the middle of the road. Lazily he contemplated the anxious faces peering at him at a safe distance behind the windscreens of the cars building up into long lines on either side of him. It would have been easy enough to drive round him, but should he have decided to charge with those dangerous, deeply-curved horns, no car would ever be the same again! Somebody had sent for the game-warden, but before the man arrived the musk-ox, taking his time, moved at a leisurely pace off the road and ambled away across the scrubby moorland of the high plateau.

This musk-ox had behaved out of character. Normally they keep well away from the roads in summer, and are more usually spotted in the distance at quieter times of the year. In the snow they are easily discernible, for unlike the majority of animals and birds that have made the North their habitat, such as the ptarmigan, the hare and the ermine, musk-oxen do not turn white or grey in winter to blend with the background. This factor, combined with the fact that when cornered they stand still in defence, made them an easy prey to man and wolf in the past, and for many years this shaggy animal, once the contemporary of the

mammoth and the sabre-toothed tiger, was extinct in Norway. Then they were reintroduced from Greenland, and have flourished on the meagre vegetation of the high plateau, needing only a sixth of the amount of food eaten by cattle. To see a mother with her calf – which even at four months weighs over 170 pounds – is a rare and marvellous sight, but at all times it is wise to use binoculars and keep well away.

We had come from Oppdal, a busy resort in both winter and summer, where we had been asked for our autographs by young children, a common request, so many of them making the collecting of tourists' signatures and foreign car numbers a hobby in the long summer holidays. In the centre of Oppdal stands an enormous troll, fashioned naturally out of a treetrunk with arms and legs. These strange formations of gnarled wood make it easy to understand the old beliefs in these mountain creatures that are so well-loved by the Norwegians, and many of these 'petrified' trolls ornament the gates of farmhouses and are set up by roadside kiosks, particularly here in the Dovre mountains, which are known to be the home of the king of all the trolls, Dovregubben, who holds court deep within, ready for any mischief as Peer Gynt found to his cost. At Vålasjø on the same Dovre plateau is a famous troll known as Dovregubben, gnarled and grotesque enough to be the true king of the trolls, looked out for by children and always good for a chuckle from the adults, since Norwegians find their trolls irresistibly funny.

Soon after Vålasjø comes Dombås, a hub of routes, which explains why it is always busy with tourist traffic, a criss-crossing of cars and caravans that have only stopped for petrol, a meal, or to re-stock from the large supermarkets there. I have always met with a cold draught at Dombås, a chill persistent breeze that has never been absent in all the countless times that I have been there, which crosses it off my list for staying any length of time.

Away to the east of Dombås lies Østerdalen, the area of broad valleys that runs parallel with the Swedish border for about 200 miles in a southward direction. One of the sights to see is the powerful River Glomma, which rises north of Røros and swirls and

28 Naihaugen, Lillehamer

tumbles for a full 370 miles before pouring out into the Oslo fjord beyond Fredrikstad. Østerdalen is renowned as being one of the best centres for the fly-fisherman, especially for the angler who rates solitude almost as high as a good catch, and the settings in which he finds himself are almost violently picture-postcard. It is a region of vast pine forests that rise and fall like the dark green swell of a mighty ocean, with 3,000 lakes, streams and rivers; it includes moorland silvery with moss and orange with cloudberries where 2,000 wild reindeer roam and peaks, ridges, and many winding roads, such as that which curls to the top of Tron at 5,500 feet above sea-level.

Mountains make a blue-grey background to the old white-painted, turf-roofed rectory of Bjørgan on the green slopes at Kvikne, the house where Bjørnstjerne Bjørnson was born in 1832. Also in Østerdalen is Elverum, a town that holds a unique place in Norway's history, for it was here in 1940 that King Håkon said the famous 'Nei!' to the German demands for a new government under Quisling. A memorial erected to his determined stand is at Leiret, the little village that was completely wiped out by German bombing, adding its name to all those other places destroyed for sheltering the King, Crown Prince and government in those dark days of April 1940.

From Dombås in a southerly direction the main road follows the great farming valley of Gudbrandsdal that opens out from the craggy heights of Mount Dovre to the north of the town and widens into gentle undulating countryside flanked to the west and east by the Jotunheimen and Rondane mountains to reach the head of Lake Mjøsa. It is a route rich in history, for pilgrims trod this way on the long journey to and from Trondheim, and they rested at farms that still bear the same names today. The old laws have always ensured the birthright of the eldest son, and even today no sizeable farm can be put up for sale without members of the family being allowed first chance to purchase.

Along this way, marching southwards from their landing point in Isfjord, came the Scottish mercenaries in 1612, led by Colonel Ramsay and Captain Sinclair. At Kringen on the slopes above the road a memorial stone depicts Pillargurie with the *lur* to her lips, the girl who sounded the long horn from the opposite mountain when the Scots reached the vital point below the piled-up trunks, rocks, and boulders set there by the local peasants. The signal sent the whole great pile a-tumbling, and the awful ambuscade sent most of the Scots to their death in the River Lågen swirling below. Those that survived were either cut down or taken prisoner; very few escaped over the mountains.

In 1940 the local people planned a similar ambuscade to halt the advance of the German forces, but the soldiers took another route, branching off at Hønefoss for Fagernes, and the plan came to nothing. There was bitter fighting at Kvam, a little south of Kringen, between the British 15th Infantry Brigade and the German forces, during which the church was burnt down. It has since been restored, and in the churchyard is a memorial to the British soldiers who fell.

In this district and at Otta there are some ancient farmhouses that have become guesthouses, and if the day is at all cool a leaping fire of crackling birch logs will make a cosy welcome to the old corner fireplace. Traditional and rustic hotels always have a *peisstue* (fireplace room) where a fire flickers to give atmosphere, drawing the guests like so many moths.

The houses, barns and byres of the farmsteads steeped in Otta's past are all of black-pitched timber with turf roofs, grouped close together in the ubiquitous traditional square, a necessary arrangement when not only did paths have to be dug in the deep snow to reach the winter-housed cattle and sheep (which is still part of the present-day agricultural scene), but their swift defence from prowling wolves meant having them within easy reach. In the onion-shaped cupola on the stabbur of these farmsteads the bell still hangs that used to ring in the workers from the fields.

Before leaving Otta it is interesting to follow the road that leads almost to the top of Pillarguriekampen, the spot where the girl on the Kringen memorial stood to blow her *lur*. The view of the valley below with its swiftly flowing river, and the snow-powdered heights of the Rondane mountains soaring to meet the sky should not be missed. When autumn touches such a scene the heather is a rich purple amid the russet, cinnamon, crimson and bitter gold of the mountains' vegetation; even the grass takes on a pinkish hue at this time of year, and the leaves of the blueberry are a pure scarlet. Between the dark pines the silver birch is a fierce yellow, but it is the mountain ash, its branches dipping under the weight of berries, that blazes like the beacons that used to raise the alarm throughout the land (the old piled stones can still be seen on many mountain tops).

Coming down to river-level again, it is often possible to spot an otter swimming with the strong current of the Lågen until, finding himself drawn towards the rapids, he will turn for the bank, and with a flick of his dark wet body disappear into the undergrowth. One of the pleasures of travelling in Norway is this constant glimpsing of all kinds of wild life. The red squirrel is extremely common, darting about in trees and at the roadside. Sometimes when the snow is late the hare in his white winter coat can be sighted easily on the autumnal slopes of the mountains.

I have often seen lemmings, which are usually stragglers left from some giant suicidal migration, charming little rodents in shades of rust, ginger, black and golden-brown, not unlike minia-ture guinea-pigs. Once on the road from Lom to Geiranger there were so many of them continually running across under the wheels of the car that it made the journey a nightmare for me. That same year Romsdal was full of them, and at Øvsteldal farm we had great difficulty in keeping them out of the cellars. They seemed quite without fear, and one even ran into the kitchen at breakfast-time, stood on its hind legs, squeaked and departed. To squeak in this way is their only defence when cornered, and they are unable to run very fast on their tiny legs, usually diving under a stone whenever possible. When that stone is lifted up they squeak in surprise, and scramble off again. To me it is one of nature's wonders that these almost legendary little creatures know that the lakes and fjords are not the ocean for which they are bound, and on they travel with that blind determination to hurl themselves into those salty depths and swim until they drown.

From Otta it is possible to branch off towards the Bøverdalen, a dramatic valley, and the immense mountains of Jotunheimen (Home of the Giants), where it is said that once the king of the frost giants, Trym, hid the hammer of the mighty Norse god, Tor, and demanded the goddess Freya in marriage in exchange for its return. But Tor disguised himself as the goddess, heavily veiled, and almost gave himself away at the pre-wedding feast by eating a whole ox and many salmon, washing it all down with three huge barrels of mead. But Trym was either gullible, or besotted by love, for he accepted the explanation that the goddess had not eaten for days in her eagerness to come to him, and he had the hammer brought into the great hall. Tor leapt up and seized it, threw off his disguise, and slew all there before flying back to Asgård, the home of the gods.

The village of Vågå has its own troll-giant (*jotun*), who in disguise as a sleigh-driver whisked home with the speed of lightning from Copenhagen a homesick local man, Johannes Blessom. When Johannes had been set down near his house the sleigh-driver bade him go indoors and not look back. But Johannes, with the insatiable curiosity of all mortals in legend and real life alike, looked back over his shoulder in time to see the mountains open to let the mysterious sleigh-driver vanish into the brilliantly lit interior. That was how Johannes knew it had been the Vågå troll-giant who had brought him home, but when he tried to straighten his neck again it proved impossible. He remained crooked-necked, looking back over his shoulder, for the rest of his life.

Vågä is an interesting village, quite apart from its legend. Standing on the banks of Lake Vågåvatn, many of its farmsteads are so ancient that several of the houses and byres have been removed to museums, and it has a spired, red-brown church that was originally a stave church, one of six in Valdres. In contrast to this time-weathered setting, there is a large heated swimming stadium in the village, which is a welcome asset to be found in many unexpected places, most of them having been paid for by funds raised for sports developments by the national lotteries.

It was in Vågå and the neighbouring village that the Scottish survivors of the ambuscade in 1612 sought refuge, and in each case they were taken into people's homes, and their wounds dressed. Some of the survivors settled down in Norway, never to return to Scotland, and one bought a patch of land in Våga and stayed there. It is still known as Skotsgård (Scot's Farm). The present buildings are of no great age, but a grassy, levelled-out place on the slopes shows where the original dwelling house stood, and down by the lake is an ancient log storehouse with a turf roof, which had been built by the hands of that Scottish survivor of Kringen.

The road from Våga leads on to Lom, where the brown-timbered stave church is particularly fine, although altered to a cruciform in the seventeenth century, the gabled roofs dragon-fanged, and the interior splendidly primitive with that scent of sweet, dry wood and summer hay that lingers in these old churches. King Olav the Saint is said to have spent a night at Lom during his travels, and the log building in which he slept is now in the local museum.

From Lom it is no great distance to Mount Galdhøpiggen, which is not only the highest mountain in the Jotunheimen, but at 8,095 feet it is the highest in Norway. At the top of it, buried in snow, is a tiny kiosk with no one in attendance, but a notice asks you to leave money in a box for any of the special badges or souvenirs that you wish to purchase. Walking tours in the Jotunheimen are very popular, and can be arranged to link up with chalets where you can stay overnight; the food is good, simple and plentiful, which is exactly what is needed after a hard day's exercise. Packed lunches can be bought, and clothing should be light and very warm, for even in July it is possible to run into a snowstorm if the weather should turn bad. That you need stout and comfortable footwear goes without saying.

The exception to this footwear rule is a pair of rubber-soled canvas shoes worn by my athletic nephew who – not having his mountain boots with him – set off for Galdhøpiggen in the first pair of shoes that came to hand. As he runs in the mountains as other people walk he suffered no hardship, but found himself the centre of interest when he stopped at a chalet for coffee. It was full of foreign walkers and climbers, all expensively booted and equipped. They stared at his canvas shoes, knowing he had just come down from the top of Galdhøpiggen. 'How do you manage in those?' asked a Dane incredulously. 'I've tried every kind of footwear in the mountains', my nephew replied, tongue in cheek, 'but these canvas shoes are the best yet!'

South of Otta lies Lillehammar, one of the loveliest resorts in Gudbrandsdal at all times of the year, lying on the softly undulating slopes above Lake Mjøsa with the river Mesna tumbling in waterfalls and swirling rapids through the centre of the town itself, overhung in parts by the flowers of the terraced cafés. One of the best open-air museums anywhere is Maihaugen, which owes its existence to a travelling dentist, Anders Sandvik, who had a great love for the folklore and culture of Gudbrandsdal, and grieved to see how old works of peasant craftsmanship were carelessly destroyed or thrown away. Often he took an ancient wooden bowl or a horn spoon in payment for his dentistry, and when finally he returned from one round of visits with a whole wagonload of old furniture it was the start of the Maihaugen museum. Now over 100 buildings are gathered together, all from Gudbrandsdal and dating back to medieval times, standing in a leafy park with lakes. Guides in the traditional costume of the county take you in and out of the old manor farms, all fully furnished, with workshops, stabburs, byres, water-mills, and the stave church that lies reflected in the blue-green depths of a lake.

A long bridge crosses Lake Mjøsa, and a road leads to the forest-covered slopes and fertile valley of Aulestad where, with the flag flying, stands the stately white house that was the home from 1875 to his death in 1910 of Bjørnstjerne Bjørnson, who in 1859 had written the words of the national anthem that were set to the music of Rikard Nordraak. Poet, playwright, author, winner of the Nobel Prize for Literature, a campaigner against injustice in all its forms, Bjørnson hated and abhorred militarism, championed freedom from dogma in religion, attacked in the world Press the oppression of minorities by powerful nations, and symbolized to countless bonded peoples the one voice crying in the wilderness. Letters of appeal, thanks, and new causes poured into the house at Aulestad, which has been preserved exactly as it was when Bjørnson lived there.

In the coach-house are the two elegant black carriages in which Bjørnson used to ride to Lillehammar railway station to meet the famous that came to visit him, such as Edvard Grieg, Jonas Lie, Alexander Kielland and Henrik Ibsen, whose son married Bjørnson's elder daughter, Bergljot. The house is full of rich gifts that Bjørnson received on many occasions during his lifetime, including a gold bowl that came full of orchids to him and his wife on their golden wedding day in 1908 from King Håkon and Queen Maud. One of the gifts he treasured most was a Norwegian flag presented to him in 1905 when the link with all foreign unions was finally broken, a gift from a fellow poet, Jonas Lie, and his wife, who had sewn it herself. 'A pure Norwegian flag at last!' Bjørnson said with deep feeling.

Bjørnson had five children, and on his study desk is a little bowl with a lid in which he used to keep candy for when his many grandchildren came to fill the house in summertime. Every morning he put a piece for each child on the edge of his desk. They would come in to greet him, take their candy, and depart. If a piece was left over he knew that one child had failed to bid him good morning. 'Nobody is so busy', he would say reprovingly, 'that he hasn't time to be polite.'

In the large kitchen is the copper pot where the hot chocolate was made for the local village children who came to visit him on Constitution Day, and to receive the cakes and sweets that he always had for them, a simple custom that spread to become a tradition throughout the land that every 17 May should be a day of children's processions and events.

After Bjørnson's death in Paris, almost his last words being: 'I turn my face towards Norway', his wife lived on at Aulestad, and wore white to the end of her days. She became known as the White Queen, and often sat under the awning on the veranda where once she and Bjørnson had gathered their family about them. The younger daughter, Dagni, is now in her late nineties and lives in Oslo, but she still visits Lillehammar and Aulestad from time to time.

North of Aulestad lies the Peer Gynt Road, a high mountain route linked to the legend of Ibsen's anti-hero, who was a farmer in this area. One of the ancient log-buildings from his farm is now used as a tourist information office.

But turning south again is to reach the shores of Lake Mjøsa where the old paddle-steamer, *Skibladner*, plies leisurely between Lillehammar and Minnesund, its wheels lapping up the water as they have done since 1858. The six hours' voyage on the largest lake in Norway gives a rolling panorama of passing scenery, and food is served on board. Otherwise there is a choice of two main routes running southwards which follow opposite sides of the lake most of the way.

The road to the west of the lake is less used by tourists, but is preferable to some for that fact alone. It passes through Gjøvik, the 'white town' that nestles on the lakeside, and also Raufoss where an ammunition factory has been scored into a mountain. In 1971 the factory celebrated with two days of festivities the 75th anniversary of its foundation with true Norwegian enthusiasm for milestones in the passage of time. There was a royal visit, the royal guards marched and the whole town fluttered with the Norwegian flag. A circus was laid on, but the highlight for everybody was the sight of one of the six aluminium motor-cars that had been built by the factory in 1920 being driven to the celebrations by the manager of the company. It was a very thin, narrow vehicle, polished and shining as though still brand-new, and the driver sat high at the wheel, looking over the head of the solitary passenger seated in front!

On the other side of the lake the E.6 passes through Hamar with its ruins of the twelfth-century cathedral where, in *Kristin Lavransdatter*, Sigrid Undset's Nobel Prize-winning novel of Norway in the Middle Ages, the child Kristin was befriended by the old monk, Brother Edvin, who showed her the glory of the new stained-glass window, and the glow of Christ's scarlet robe fell full upon her.

In Hamar railway enthusiasts of all ages enjoy the railway museum, and pile into the Lilliput train for the short ride. There are old carriages and rolling stock to be viewed, and a quaint little wooden station named Kløften. The black-funnelled, blue-green engine 'Caroline' chuffs her way up and down the track and the largest engine is old 'Dovregubben', the name of the king of the trolls, which was built to take the haul over the Dovre mountains. In Hamar itself all the present railway stock of Norway is serviced and maintained.

To the east of the road at Eidsvold there stand the large white building with flag flying where the constitution was signed in 1814. After that it is not long before a large sign at the roadside announces that you have entered the boundaries of Oslo.

8. Østfold and Vestfold

On the east shores of Oslo fjord lies Østfold, the county that is half covered by forest. Its rolling farmland, rich and fertile, is cut through by the great river Glomma, which bears floating logs southwards from distant Østerdalen to their destination at the wood-processing factories of Fredrikstad and Sarpsborg.

The county's eastern boundary meets the Swedish border, but along its coast are the islands, sounds, inlets, and coves that, with the county of Vestfold on the fjord's west shore, make Oslo fjord a magnet for those seeking bathing beaches, bathing rocks, and idyllic sailing conditions. Everywhere in Østfold and Vestfold are the cottages and summer homes, many perching at the water's edge, of Norwegians who rejoice in the sea air. Almost everybody has a boat.

In July and August the Oslo fjord often reaches a sea-temperature of 21°C, and there is very little tide, no more than one and a half feet between high and lower water; moreover the *solgang-bris*, which means 'the breeze that follows the sun', enables local yachtsmen to forecast exactly when the wind will change on at least eight days out of every ten. In summer international regattas are held, and the yachtsmen compete for the King Olav Cup among other coveted trophies. Hankø, an island off the shores of Østfold, is known as the Cowes of the North, and Norway's sea-loving King himself has a summer villa there. The sun-drenched rocks on the island are full of spots to picnic or sun-bathe while watching the racing yachts go skimming by.

In these waters sailed the ships of earlier sun-worshippers –

those of the Bronze Age. In the summer of 1971 one of these primitive craft was to be seen again for the first time for 2,500 years, a crew of young men at the oars. Professor Sverre Marstrander, who had spent 17 years studying the rock carvings of these strange, almost mythical dragon- and horse-headed ships, supervised the design, building and testing of the vessel. This exact replica of wood and hide, with its unique keel extending fore and aft, was built at Fredrikstad by a local boat-builder, who used only the materials available to Bronze Age man. The sturdy wooden curve of the unusual double prow proved to be extremely effective when beaching in protecting from damage the comparatively fragile lashed hides of the flat-bottom craft, and this forerunner of the Viking ships showed itself to be eminently seaworthy. It has been said jokingly that Thor Heyerdahl, who has been so far afield in replicas of ancient craft, overlooked the chance of this exciting venture on his own doorstep.

On Highway 110 between Sarpsborg and Fredrikstad there are rock-carvings of these Bronze Age ships, some of them appearing to carry the sun on its journey. Among other prehistoric finds of exceptional interest along this 'Road of Antiquities' are the circles of great stones that stretch away up the hills, once used in some long-lost ritual, and burial mounds that date back 3,000 years. Right by the barrows is the original 2,000-year-old Ancient Road, and it is possible to follow its grass-covered deep indentation for some distance. Not far from here is Storedal farm where King Magnus the Blind was born; it is now the site of a modern school for the blind.

Sarpsborg is one of Østfold's most important industrial and export harbours with the largest wood-processing enterprise in Norway and two great power stations that supply the many factories. It is enriched by the River Glomma that brings to it the logs from the distant forests of the eastern valleys, and tumbles in a 64-feet drop of roaring, cascading water through the heart of the town. It was this spectacular waterfall, known as Sarpsfoss, that caused King Olav the Saint to stay his ship as he sailed up the Glomma while he gazed at it with the same pleasurable awe with which visitors regard it today. On his orders a fortress and a church were built there, and afterwards it became the winter quarters of the Viking kings.

The sawmills of the sixteenth century founded the town's industrial life, and even today the statue of a logger in the centre of the busy market-place personifies the heart-beat of Sarpsborg. I once had to deliver a parcel for a friend in Sarpsborg, and drove for seemingly endless miles past stacked timber in a kind of golden-brown maze made noisy with sawmills before emerging again and finding the right road. This took me near the spacious, strikingly designed Sparta Stadium, one of the many amenities enjoyed by the population of this thriving, prosperous town with its abundance of sculpture, parks, gardens, and freshwater bathing spots. Its background of thick dark forest gives it every right to call itself Østfold's 'garden city'. The old Manor Houses of Hafslund and Borregaard bear graceful witness to the prosperity and culture of earlier times, and for gardeners the collection of medicinal herbs from medieval times in the grounds of Borgarsyssel Museum is of exceptional interest. It is here in Borgarsyssel, Østfold's county museum, that Professor Marstrander's replica of the Bronze Age sun-worshippers' ship is magnificently housed.

On the E.6 from Sarpsborg it is only a short distance to the 1,475-feet long Svinnesund Bridge that spans the lovely Iddefjord, which makes a natural barrier between Norway and Sweden at this point. Many Norwegians swam this wide stretch of water at all times of the year during the German Occupation in a desperate attempt to reach freedom in neutral Sweden. This part of the country has always been actively involved in times of conflict, and the seventeenth-century fortress of Fredriksten at Halden, overlooking the fjord, faced many Swedish attacks, but was never taken. During a siege of the town during the Great Nordic War (1709–21) King Karl XII of Sweden met his death, and in the park named after him a pillar stands on the spot where he fell. The old fortress is in an excellent state of preservation: ornamented archways lead into quiet, sun-filled courtyards with the dark gleam of antique cannon. In the old arsenal is the original tavern where today's visitors, after scanning the wide view from the ramparts, can take some refreshment.

Halden is an industrial town, producing 20 per cent of Norway's footwear as well as having large timber-processing factories, but contrasting with its splendidly designed up-to-date factories are the old houses in the narrow streets with the characteristic *midtark* roofs that are flat and sloping in the middle, the white Empire-style Immanuels Church with its cross on the square tower rising high against the blue skies, and the unusual semi-circular covered bazaar, hung with trade signs, in the market-place. Halden is also a centre for nuclear research, no less than 13 nations working together at the atomic reactor situated – its safety is 100 per cent guaranteed – in the very heart of the town. Another atomic centre is at Kjeller, near Oslo.

If Halden means shoes and atomic research to most Norwegians then the town of Fredrikstad, divided into eastern and western parts by the River Glomma flowing out into the fjord, means one of Norway's top football teams. But it is here that tankers of 100,000 tons are built, and ship-building with a host of other industries has made Fredrikstad one of Norway's most important centres.

Yet the Old Town on the eastern bank, dating from 1567 when King Frederik II founded the place that was to bear his name, seems as cut off by the centuries as by the river and moats that surround it, particularly on a Sunday when the vast cobbled square with the wooden stocks, as well as the picturesque narrow streets, are almost deserted. Most people prefer to visit on weekdays when PLUS, the centre of Norwegian Applied Art, is open to visitors. Then the weavers, the glass-blowers, the potters, and many other artists and craftsmen can be seen at work in the studios and workshops housed in the old buildings unchanged since the seventeenth and eighteenth centuries. The works of art and goods produced are among the best to be had anywhere, creating an exciting blaze of colour and a blending of interesting surfaces and textures against the ancient wooden walls of this unique centre. Here within the star-shaped ramparts of the Old Town, approached by pedestrians across the ancient drawbridge, are the ornate archways, the rows of black cannon, and the great cobbled courtyards that once rang to the marching feet of the scarlet-coated soldiery in tricorne hats.

It is a pity that the town of Moss, which is linked so conveniently by ferry to Vestfold on the opposite side of the fjord, should frequently be subject to the unpleasant aroma that drifts from its particular factories and discourage any inclination to stay and explore for a while. It has many interesting old buildings, and once played an important role in Norway's history. It was here on 14 August 1814, at the Moss Convention, that the union between Norway and Sweden was settled, allowing Norway to remain an independent nation under the Swedish crown, a state of affairs that was to last until 1905. The meeting of ministers was in the eighteenth-century mansion that belonged to the Moss Iron Works, known ever since as Konventiongården, a large, graceful building, painted yellow, its rococo woodwork picked out in white. It stands in the part of the town known as Verket, and in Verksgaten (Works Street) are the ancient rust-red wooden houses that were built to accommodate the hands at the iron works.

Inland, away from the fjord, Østland is full of lakes and rivers set amid rolling farmland and scattered hamlets, ideal for those able to take a canoe or a small boat with the car. At Otteid a canal boat travels far into Sweden through scenery that is delightful and unspoilt, but not spectacular.

Yet it is the coastal area that attracts the majority of holiday-makers, the whole stretch being full of villages and hamlets, many of them linked to the old sailing-ship days, such as Son, north of Moss, with 530 inhabitants and quaint old houses from the sixteenth, seventeenth and eighteenth centuries. It has always attracted artists, but none has put the hamlet on the map as much as Karl Dørnberger, who was born in Norway in 1864 of German parentage. His house, now a private residence, stands at the water's edge in Nedre Strandgade, a grand crest above the upper window. He moved into it in 1907, and lived there until his death in 1940. It looks peaceful enough today, but in Karl Dørnberger's time it was guarded by savage dogs, and hidden gun-traps in the garden deterred anyone from making an unlawful entry. But local people and summer visitors alike were only too anxious to avoid all contact with the eccentric painter, who liked to refer to himself as 'the last Musketeer'.

Dørnberger was a huge man with a bellowing voice, who stumped about on a wooden leg and wore pistols at his belt. He was a great practical joker, and liked to alarm fellow passengers on trains by flourishing a knife, and then driving it through his trouser-leg into his wooden stump as though into his own flesh ! In his house unsuspecting guests were treated to a number of unpleasant surprises, which included coming face to face with a suit of armour, the arm of which would shoot up suddenly to shake a vicious-looking spiked battle-axe at them. In his kitchen the artist had a collection of skulls and Black Magic paraphernalia, and word of this added to the house's dark reputation. Karl Dørnberger will not soon be forgotten in peaceful little Son.

Vestfold on the west side of the fjord is Norway's smallest county. It has a similar landscape to Østfold, and the whole area has been inhabited ever since the great inland ice mass melted northwards, evidence of its retreat left in the morraine of stone and gravel that can be sighted while wandering on both sides of Oslo Fjord. Vestfold with its woods, rocks, and farmland slides away to blend into the mountains of the neighbouring county of Telemark, and rivals Østfold in its abundance of holiday coves, bathing resorts and fast-growing light industries.

From Oslo the E.18 leads to Vestfold by way of Asker, village of Skaugum, the residence of the Crown Prince and Princess, and the church where King Olav's two daughters, Princesses Ragnhild and Astrid, were married. Then the highway leads on through the timber and ship-building town of Drammen, situated on the mouth of the river of the same name, and it is an old local boast to say that 'an hour in Drammen is better than a dram in an hour'. Leaving aside the alcoholic implication, an hour or so in Drammen can be well spent in driving or taking an excursion up the brightly-lit tunnel road called The Spiral, which curls in six spirals right up

29 *Seljord church,
Telemark, from
the west*

30 *East end of Lake Totak, Telemark*

to the top of the forest-clad heights of Bragernesåsen above the town, where a panoramic view spreads out over the slopes of Eiker and the lovely Mjøndalen, a stretch of misty blues and greens shading to pine-black and indigo.

Crossing the county border into Vestfold the highway passes by steep hills and through small villages much favoured by artists and writers. At Horten the ferry links with Moss in Østfold and sees a continual stream of traffic at all times of the year. It is known that a regular ferry service operated here as early as 1582, and there is every reason to believe that it was in existence at least a hundred years before that; then it would have taken a great deal longer to cross at this narrowest point between Vestfold and Østfold than the 45 minutes of the brand-new car ferries in use today.

Horten became Norway's premier naval base in 1815 (the distinction now belongs to Bergen) and a road through a chestnut grove leads to the bridge spanning a truly picturesque canal and the entrance to the old naval establishment, Karl Johansvern. For adults and children alike interested in ships it is worth a visit; the Naval Museum includes Norway's oldest torpedo boat as well as replicas of the Gokstad Viking ship, the frigate *Freia*, and many others. The last Norwegian–Swedish Union flag is displayed here, and also the first royal flag that was run up for King Håkon VII when he landed in Norway in 1905.

The first Norwegian to be killed in the German invasion in 1940 was a naval man, Captain Leif Welding, and a memorial statue of him stands in Horten. Another in the birch grove by the library is of the Polar explorer, Oscar Wisting, and his faithful dog Obersten (Colonel), for Horten has long had connections with polar expeditions. Three of its men went with Wisting when he accompanied Roald Amundsen to the South Pole, and forestalled Captain Scott by such a brief space of time.

In Borre Nature Park, just over two miles from Horten, is a collection of 29 huge burial mounds in which lie the Ynglinge kings and queens who claimed descent from Odin himself, and whose blood ran in the veins of all the great Viking kings. The

31   The Folk Museum, Eidsborg

Ynglinge King Halvdan moved his court to the Horten area in A.D. 800, and Snorre, the chronicler, tells in the sagas that this king, who was the grandfather of Harald Fairhair, lies buried at Borre. The building of a road in 1850, just below the twelfth-century church, inadvertently destroyed a barrow, revealing that a Viking burial ship had lain there. Only a small part of the find was salvaged, but it was enough to date the barrow at 900 and to show that it had been as well supplied with grave-goods as the Oseberg and Gokstad Viking ships, both of which were uncovered in Vestfold.

A side road off the E.18 leads to the wholly charming little resort of Åsgårdstrand. There is a certain magic in wandering down the steeply sloping village street, past the neat wooden houses in their flower-filled gardens and on to the bridge, there to lean on the rails, and see how unchanged the setting is since Munch painted his famous picture 'Girls on the Bridge' in 1899. The tall trees still fill the sky with foliage at the water's edge and the boxy whiteness of the large house, Kiøsterudgarden, looms there as it does in the painting's background.

At Åsgårdstrand Munch lived in a humble yellow-painted house where the simply furnished interior has been kept exactly as it was when he slept in the narrow bed with the rust-coloured spread and took his breakfast by the window. The house is built on a slope with the front door opening into the lane, and the rear door with wooden steps leads to a tree-shaded lawn that stretches down to the water's edge with a view of the islands and skerries. His studio, which was taken down after his death in 1944, has been reconstructed on its original site by the house. In this garden Munch met the girl that he wanted to marry, but her father forbade the match, and destroyed the paintings that the artist had given her.

No doubt the village was a gossipy place in Munch's time, and behind lace curtains curious eyes watched the handsome artist's comings and goings, and the women he entertained in the house. One day Munch knocked down with a blow on the chin a man who accused him of being immoral, one of many incidents in his own life that he committed to canvas. This picture can now be seen in the Munch Museum in Oslo.

Munch found it easy to work at Åsgårdstrand. He said of his house that it was the only home-like place that he had ever lived in, and apart from producing some of his best paintings there he drew the first drafts for 'The Frieze of Life' at Åsgårdstrand, as well as those for the magnificent murals that grace the Freia chocolate factory.

Continuing towards Tønsberg you see first of all the square tower of Slottsfjellet on the hill overlooking the town. It was raised a hundred years ago in 1870 to mark the 1,000th anniversary of Tønsberg's foundation, and it stands amid the ruins of the twelfth-century Mikael Church and those of a thirteenth-century citadel and Tunsberghus Castle. Tønsberg is the oldest town in Norway, older than the kingdom itself, for the sagas tell that the Viking king, Harald Fairhair, rested in the market-place there before claiming it in his unification of all Norway.

The charming Norwegian nursery rhyme 'Ride, ride erect, the horse named Blanka' is believed to have originated in Tønsberg, sung by Queen Blanka to her baby son as she dandled him on her lap. In 1335 she had come as a very young girl to Tønsberg to marry the 18-year-old King Magnus Eriksson in the Mikael Church on Slottsfjellet, after which she lived with him there in the citadel.

Two local men have also made their mark on the town's history. Svend Foyn, whose home near the red stone cathedral is now a home for elderly women, invented the shell harpoon in 1873 and revolutionized the whale-catching industry in which the town was deeply involved. Its other great source of income was from shipping, and Wilhelm Wilhelmsen changed his Tønsberg fleet from sail to steam, putting it at the forefront of the world at that time. Wilhelmsen's very grand residence, pink-tinted, stands in a wide spread of lawn and is now the town hall.

The prosperity of Tønsberg today is evident in the expensive power-boats and yachts that bob at local moorings, and in the strikingly designed houses that stand in their own grounds amid the natural beauty of wooded countryside that makes up the suburbs (Norwegian architects make sure that builders do not 'clear' sites, but try to preserve all the trees already there). Affluence is also reflected in all the new buildings of the town, which include the 'Klubben' with its attractive nautical décor reminiscent of windjammer days, and the enormous shopping centre with a new and startling abstract sculpture in the forecourt representing the sea-going spirit of Tønsberg, all built – as with every new building in Norway – of the very best quality materials, ensuring that time will not cause any kind of deterioration to spoil their shining splendour.

The old parts of Tønsberg consist of narrow streets lined with mellow wooden houses, many hung with creeper, an area almost maze-like, for the streets wander into each other and criss-cross in the most confusing way, making it very easy to lose one's sense of direction and end up time and time again in the market-place or by the sea. The pedestrian does well to arm himself with a town map, but the young tourist pilots are there for the motorists, sitting astride their scooters as they wait by the Vestfold Museum, where a full-scale replica of the prow of the Oseberg Viking ship, which was found near Tønsberg, soars skywards by the entrance. The museum houses the town's whaling and maritime history collection, and includes the skeletons of several whales, including that of a Blue whale 75 feet long. The open-air section has a special charm, for here Vestfold farmhouses, byres and stabburs are set amid trees on the grassy slopes, and you are free to wander in and out with no ropes to keep you back from close inspection of the fine old furniture, the collection of ancient saddles, the chests, the tapestries and the spinning-wheels.

The saeter café serves rustic dishes, and it is extremely pleasant to sit at a wooden table outside in the sun with a plate of rømmegrøt sprinkled with cinnamon and sugar, gleaming with golden butter, with a glass of cold milk to round off the simple meal that must have appeared innumerable times on the great pine tables in the farmhouses that have just been visited.

Tønsberg is at the centre of many popular bathing places on both islands and mainland where the beaches are never crowded, trees give pleasant shade, and parking is free, as it is almost everywhere in Norway except in the main streets of the larger cities. On the tip of the island of Tjøme is Verdens Ende (The End of the World), which is approached by a leafy lane that leads to a stretch of smooth and wonderfully rounded rocks linked by a stone jetty with diving boards, making it possible to walk some distance out to sea and find a secluded corner all to yourself. Of particular interest is the ancient beacon that stands on a high point, the iron basket on the long prop having once been stuffed with rags soaked in fish-oil to blaze in warning of the rocks to ships sailing past.

There used to be great rivalry between the whalers of Tønsberg and the near-by town of Sandefjord, but those days have gone, together with the spectacular setting-out of the whaling fleets for the starting of the season in the Antarctic. Sandefjord is now primarily a shipping town, but the whalers of the past are remembered in the magnificent revolving monument set like a jewel in a vast lawn- and tree-enhanced square by the sea. Amid fountains of water that rise and fall like the waves of a sea a slim rowing-boat perches precariously on the back of a rising whale, the harpoonist poised high in the tilted prow as he aims his slender, hand-thrown weapon at the quarry while his companions struggle at the oars.

All along the coast the prawn boats offer their freshly-cooked catches for sale, and hotels and restaurants make a feature of rosy mountains of prawns on the famous cold tables where you can help yourself as many times as you wish. In private homes prawn suppers with white wine, crusty new bread, farm butter, and home-made mayonnaise make a meal that is not easily forgotten by the overseas visitor lucky enough to be invited to one. There was a time for three weeks every July at the height of the holiday season when it was impossible to buy fresh prawns. 'The prawn fishermen want their holiday with everyone else,' I was told in explanation, but I am thankful to say that these holidays are now staggered, and a bagful of this pink harvest of the sea contributes to many a splendid picnic eaten by the shore, although it is quite likely that the local village baker will have a notice on his door 'Closed for three weeks'. The Norwegians value their holidays, and know that trade will be waiting when they return again.

In contrast to the multi-coloured little towns in other parts of Norway, white paint predominates throughout these southern parts, although by tradition the barn is always painted rust-red. Passing through the fertile countryside you see neat white farmhouses gleaming in the sun, and in some towns, such as Larvik, lying south of Sandefjord, whole streets shine with the same scrubbed whiteness.

Larvik, birthplace of Thor Heyerdahl, whose charming childhood home still stands in Stengate, has for its crest a beech-tree, for all around lies the largest beech forest in Norway – a rare tree here in the north – and in it are over a hundred burial mounds from Viking times. The town, which has been a timber and fishing port for a long time, stands in a bay where the fjord sweeps out into the waters of the Skagerrak.

The core of the town was once destroyed by fire and rebuilt with a great deal of square concrete, but the past lingers hauntingly in the ancient customs house on the wharf and in the Manor House, known as Herregården, with its richly decorated salons, that was built for the first governor of the town, the Danish Duke Ulrik Frederik Gyldenløve. Larvik calls itself Gyldenløve's Town and on 29 September 1971 celebrated with a great many festivities the 300th anniversary of its foundation. Herregården, enlarged later by Gyldenløve's son into the stately three-storied, red-painted wooden mansion that it is today, was made ready in 1677 in time for the Danish governor to take his bride home after their marriage in Trinity Church, which had also been built at his instructions. The paintings in the church are of exceptional interest, especially 'Suffer little children to come unto me' by the German painter Lucas Cranach (1472–1553). Next to the church is the hospital, a long, low white building with a red roof that has been a home for elderly women ever since it was given jointly to the town in 1792 by the widowed Queen Anne Sophie of Denmark and two Danish dukes.

Only five miles away from Larvik is the lovely little village of Stavern, which came into prominence during the eighteenth century when Frederik v had a naval base built there. It was well known to Norway's great sea-hero, Tordenskjold, whose statue by Gustav Vigeland, set in open lawns approached by way of Havnegaten, shows him with his coat flapping in the breeze as he gazes towards the sea and the little citadel island with the harbour that he used so often during the Great Nordic War. Today the island with its fortress (built by Gyldenløve) is as full of artists as it was once of Tordenskjold's seamen.

Another link with the sea is the grey stone pyramid-shaped building high on the hill above Stavern. This is the memorial to Norwegian seamen of both world wars, and in its hall are hundreds and hundreds of names that bear witness to the heavy toll that was taken by the German navy even in the years 1914–18 when Norway was neutral. From the steps of the memorial there is a fine view over Fredriksvern Wharf with its star-shaped ramparts, old cannon and 17 buildings from the eighteenth century, used now as an Air Force Training School. The gates, topped by the monogram of Frederik v, are always open, for they offer the quickest way to one of the popular bathing beaches where swimmers and sunbathers gather on the long summer days, and the coloured sails drift feather-like between the islands.

Other places to stroll in include the park where four quaint old water-pumps, painted white, dating from the naval-base days, stand enclosed by curved balustrades, graceful as Grecian columns; also there is the way through the market-place to the garrison church, built in 1756, the bright ochre and rust-red paint of its outside walls setting off with a slightly bizarre touch the ornate rococo entrance and interior. In the churchyard lies the poet, Jonas Lie, and his wife Thomasine, who made the 'pure' Norwegian flag with her own hands for Bjørnstjerne Bjørnson. A pond with waterlilies reflects the church's waisted steeple, and on a mound of rounded stones amid a rippling fountain sits the sculptured little 'Stavern boy'.

South of Stavern it is not far to the county border where Vestfold meets Telemark and the Norwegian Riviera. The 'windjammer' atmosphere lingers on along the coast, but inland the centuries turn back even further.

9. The South Coast and Telemark

Kristiansand is the port that opens the way to Norway for many visitors. It lies almost at the central tip of the coastal strip of the South land, often called the Norwegian Riviera, that stretches for more than 200 miles from Vestfold and the mouth of the Oslo Fjord in the east to just south of Stavanger in the west. It is an area of sandy beaches, smooth rocks and hundreds of lovely little islands. Nowhere is crowded, not even at the height of the summer season, and often the water is so clear that you can see the fish swimming in the sun-shot depths far below. The Gulf Stream ensures that the sea-temperature is as high as anywhere else in Europe short of the Mediterranean.

Backed by softly rolling wooded hills, its quaysides always busy with shipping, the predominantly white, grey, and rust-red town of Kristiansand, speared by the copper spire of its cathedral, owes the grid plan of its streets to Christian IV, who took a keen interest in his Norwegian domain, and supervised in 1641 the building of the town named after him, very much as he had replanned Oslo after the great fire a few years earlier. There was a settlement on this site centuries before, a fact borne out by the tall rune stone in the Oddernes churchyard. The runic inscription states that the church was built, in 1040, by Eyvind, godson of Saint Olav, on his own land.

There is the same salty atmosphere about Kristiansand as there is about Bergen. The fish-market also offers live fish in troughs, and there is a busy trade in bags of prawns, which people often buy for an immediate snack. For a long time in one of the troughs there was a particular cod that for some reason had been spared the knife, and it became quite a local pet, and a great favourite with the children, who fed tit-bits into its eager, gaping mouth. Unlike Bergen Kristiansand has little of interest in its history. The Christiansholm Fortress, founded in 1674, has a dramatic show of old cannon on its rotunda, but only once were they ever fired. That was a volley aimed at a British warship during the Napoleonic Wars. The volley was not returned, and the warship departed.

Kristiansand has much to commend it and is a good centre from which to explore the surrounding countryside and villages. It is not only railway enthusiasts who enjoy the three-mile trip on the steam train preserved by the Setesdal Railway Hobby Club, which is run every Sunday in the summer by club members who spend their spare time polishing, cleaning and repairing the railway's rolling stock. The engine was built in Scotland in 1895 and runs from Grovane to Beihølen, passing through woods and by the river Otra, over a bridge, round sharp curves, into tunnels and out again. Stops are made for taking photographs and buying refreshments in the old restaurant car; extra stops are made when passengers want to get out and pick the lilies-of-the-valley that spread in a white carpet by the tracks, and there is another halt if the engine-driver loses his cap and has to jump out to retrieve it!

An enjoyable way to visit a number of the small villages lying to the east of Kristiansand is to take the 50-year-old boat *Øya* as she plies her route between the skerries, throbbing along at a comfortable speed of eight knots, carrying everything from a wood-stove for a summer cottage to goods for a local shop, and perhaps a crate of bottles ordered from one of the state-owned Vinmonopol branches. In the natural harbours, creeks and bays of these small islands the windjammers used to be moored stem to stern, and many of the old mooring-rings still remain in the stone walls. Lillesand was the first place in Norway where people started to board the black timbers of the old houses, and then paint them in various colours. White was the most expensive paint of all, and gradually it became a status symbol with prosperous sea-faring men to have white-painted houses, a whim that spread to make white traditional in the southernmost regions of Norway.

Many of these mariners' houses date from the eighteenth and early nineteenth century, charmingly ornate with verandahs, balconies and woodwork as delicate as lace. To one of them, called Skrivergården, came an Irishman, Robert Major, who had left Belfast in 1800 after taking part in an uprising, and in 1830 he started a tannery in Lillesand.

Travelling on by road up the coast you pass the porticoed home of the 1918 Nobel Prize-winning author Knut Hamsun, who wrote *The Earth's Harvest, August* and *Life's Play*. A bust of him stands on a plinth on the sloping lawn of the house that he bought with the prize-money, looking across at a view of glinting water.

Grimstad, another old windjammer town facing a spread of beautiful skerries, also has literary associations. Down its steep, narrow streets once walked a vigorous young apothecary's assistant whose name was Henrik Ibsen. He had come to Grimstad from his birthplace, Skien. The house where he lived and worked is now a museum, and in the little room behind the shop, which is preserved with its counter and ancient bottles and pill-drawers, he wrote his first play *Catiline*, which was published in 1850. Also in Grimstad he had an unfortunate love affair that resulted in the girl bearing the 18-year-old Ibsen an illegitimate son, for whom he paid a paternity allowance for the next 14 years. In a cork drawer in the shop Ibsen carved his name on the day he left Grimstad for ever, and it can still be seen: Henr. J. Ibsen, 15.4.50.

Today Grimstad is known for its preserving industry and fruit wines, but if you follow the little road that winds in and out eastwards away from the quay you will come to an old maroon-coloured boat-house, and along the side of it are the name-plates of 33 of the ships built there from the year 1848–99, a fascinating link with those old days of sail and early steam.

Not far from Grimstad is Fjaere Church where a memorial stone has been raised to one of Norway's heroes, Terje Vigen, who has been immortalized in Ibsen's famous poem, the first lines of which can be quoted by every Norwegian at the drop of a hat. All alone Terje Vigen rowed in a small boat to Denmark to fetch food for starving families in the Napoleonic wars when the British were blockading Norway. Fjaere Church itself is one of the oldest in the country, and in the vaults are the perfectly embalmed bodies of two Viking giants, one over seven feet tall with the hands of a child; but they are not on view to the public any longer, and have been left to 'rest undisturbed'. There are windows only on the south side of the church, and in the light sat the male parishioners. The women, being of Eve who tempted Adam to his fall, had to sit on the colder, darker side of the church. In those days the men always came fully armed to church with a great clatter of swords and shields, for there was the constant danger of meeting wild animals on the way, and always the chance of enemy raiders making a surprise attack. The peasant-wrought ornamentation is worth coming a long way to see; the angels and apostles are executed with a child-like simplicity and the gates of the pews under the unusual double gallery bear the names of families who occupied them, painted in by some local hand early in the eighteenth century.

Among the resorts much favoured by artists past and present is Arendal, the hilly town embracing its harbour where once 400 windjammers used to lie at anchor; also Kragerø, which nestles amid clustered trees and rugged rocks. Both places are well used to the weekend exodus of families setting out with sail, outboard motor or by taxi-boat to their cottages on the many islands and holms that shelter the mainland. Edvard Munch came to Kragerø in 1909 and found inspiration for the murals for Oslo University's Aula. It was the mid-winter sun at Kragerø, lying low over the fjord in all its glorious colours of rose, crimson, orange, and gold that he portrayed in the centre painting, 'The Sun'. A local sailor, Borre Eriksen, was the model that Munch used for the old blind man in 'History', and the small boy who listened so attentively to the tales being told, the two figures symbolizing the past and future, is today a Kragerø businessman.

The region of Setesdal, although lying inland, is considered part of the south coast, and is known as 'the enchanted valley' because in the past its difficult terrain kept it singularly cut off from the rest of Norway, resulting in the preservation of many ancient traditions and customs that might otherwise have been lost. In the music, architecture and costume of Setesdal there remain close links with the Middle Ages, which greatly enriches the country's folklore and culture. It is still possible to glimpse an elderly woman wearing the full white-skirted, black-braided costume with a black bolero and head-dress that was once the workaday costume of all Setesdal women, but this is a rare sight, and on the whole – as in the rest of Norway – the colourful festive costumes only appear on Constitution Day, at weddings, baptisms and on other occasions of importance.

Nothing gives a better idea of the barriers that kept Setesdal enclosed than the high perpendicular mountain cliff at Fånefjell where there are three roads. The ancient one is the bridlepath that wanders far away to follow a gentler slope; the second is the later gravel road cut into the rock face and encircling the whole cliff just above the water to reach the other side; the third is the modern road that sweeps through the 600-yard-long tunnel with a fine metalled surface.

It was the railway that opened up Setesdal in 1896 but in recent years it proved uneconomical and was closed in 1962, letting the comfortable long-distance buses, also owned by the National State Railways, take over the route. The only surviving section of the railway is that run by the Setesdal Hobby Club. It does mean that at Evje, a junction for roads running to Kristiansand, Arendal and Hovden, the old railway station with its pie-frill roof stands oddly high and dry in the centre of the village with not the gleam of a track in sight. Lawns have taken over and make the kind of Walt Disney setting for the shops now housed in its waiting-rooms and ticket offices.

To continue northwards along this beautiful valley, a realm of forest and waterfall, shimmering lakes and sweeping mountains, is to reach the point where the Otra river becomes the 21-mile-long inland Byglandsfjord, popular for fishing 'dwarf' salmon. Here under the pines on tiny grass-covered spits of land thick with wild flowers, are some of the most idyllic picnic spots in the world. No sound except birds twittering, and not a breeze to stir the branches. No traffic. No sign of anyone else. Only the clear water showing the white stones far below the surface, and as the fish jump, the glittering ripples dancing away to the forest-fringed shores on the far side. At the hamlet of Bygland the white-painted church is from 1638 and in the churchyard lie the seven graves of the British and Canadian crew of an Allied aircraft brought down in 1941.

Setesdal has become known not only for its silverware, but for the particular coloured stones found in the area. They are highly valued when set in rings, brooches, and other jewellery, and can be purchased from silversmiths' workshops, which are often old timbered buildings near the roadside.

The thick foliage of the trees in summer makes it necessary to leave the road or cross the Ose bridge on to the far bank in order to get a good view of Reiarfossen, the high waterfall that comes cascading down the mountainside. Only then is it possible to picture fully the dramatic incident that resulted in it being named after the young man who jumped that terrifying stretch of water on horseback at the point where it starts its head-spinning fall. He had fallen in love with the daughter of a prosperous farmer, who intended a better match for her, but in spite of parental opposition the girl had her heart set on marrying her poor suitor. Finally the farmer cunningly agreed that Reiar should marry his daughter if he could jump a horse across the fall. It was considered to be an impossible feat, but Reiar accepted the challenge, and a crowd of local people gathered to watch the event. Reiar's horse cleared the fall, and a great cheer went up. The girl was his! But Reiar, flushed with triumph, light-headed with success, wheeled his horse about, and took the jump back again. This time the horse missed its footing, and rider and mount went crashing down those thundering falls to their death.

Further on at Flateland a side road leads up the hill to the sixteenth-century Rygnestad Farm that was once owned by the famous outlaw, Vond Åsmund, who lived from 1540 to 1610. The farmer leaves his haymaking to show visitors round the buildings – all turf-roofed, built of weather-mellowed brown timbers, furnished and equipped, giving a complete picture of farm life in the outlaw's time. The corn mill, smithy, barn, stables and byre are all intact. Part of the farmhouse, a large room with an earth floor, actually dates back to the twelfth century; the square opening was used as a chimney for the central hearth and also as a source of light, as there are no windows. It was still in use within living memory, as well as the rest of the house with its built-in wall beds; indeed the farmer's wife, a member of the Rygnestad family, was born there before the farmstead and its contents were bought for the nation in 1920. Her famous ancestor, Vond Åsmund, must have been as romantic and passionate a lover as Reiar of the waterfall at Ose, for it was the abduction of a bride that caused him to be outlawed. He had been serving as a mercenary in Holland and returned home on the day that the girl to whom he had been betrothed was about to be married to someone else. He literally snatched her away from the altar and took her to his farm.

The Thing condemned him for his action, and the local keepers of the peace came to take him in charge, but as can be seen the farm occupies a strategic position in the hillside that made defence easy, and from the gallery of the 'Nyeloft', the stabbur building that is one of the biggest in the valley (its timbers are enormous), Vond Åsmund drove them away with arrows shot with the deadly aim he had acquired during his service in foreign wars. Eventually he was pardoned, and became a rich farmer and a keeper of the peace himself. In the Nyeloft where once he stored his arms, the lower floor being used later for the more customary storage of corn, meal and flatbread, there are still in the upper storey some of the treasures that he brought back from his travels. It means mounting a flight of very difficult steps to reach the gallery and the treasure room, but it is well worth it to see the sixteenth-century Dutch glass, tapestries, and carvings, which include a bed; most interesting of all is the faded painting of Queen

Elizabeth I, Mary Stuart and Philip of Spain, standing side by side. The traditional costumes of the Rygnestad family are hung on racks, the Sunday garments vivid with braid and ornamentation contrasting with the strangely dramatic black-and-white everyday wear; the men's trousers have seats reinforced with leather, for a great deal of time was spent in the saddle.

Along the hillside between Flateland and the hamlet of Bykle runs the old Bykle Way, which was the only thoroughfare for travellers until less than a hundred years ago. Bykle itself is rich in ancient houses, and its church, which is the oldest in Setesdal, is also one of the smallest in Norway. It has only one doorway, and is remarkable for its superb rustic 'rose' painting by a local man, Vasshus, who in 1826 covered the whole interior to make it bloom like a garden. The church dates back to the eleventh century, for in spite of the enormous difficulties of travel in these parts and Setesdal's isolation as a result of it, Christianity was firmly established in Bykle as early as 1050, as revealed by some runic characters carved into a cave in Stodhedder in the uplands around the hamlet.

Bykle is steeped in legend. It is said that the original site chosen for the church was some distance away, and the heavy timbers had been placed there in readiness for commencing the building of it the following day. During the night these were transported by 'underground beings' to the centre of Bykle. Nobody dared to oppose this high-handed action, for who knew what might happen if the timbers were defiantly carted back again, and so the church, in spite of later reconstruction, stands on the same site today.

On the ceiling, above the blossoming walls of the interior and the gallery where carved white roses nestle against the rust-red lattice-work, Christ gazes down amid clouds and stars. An attempt was made to destroy some of the paintings between 1864 and 1880 by the priest there at that time. He resented the fact that his congregation allowed their eyes to wander over the church's splendour during his sermons, and failed to keep their attention glued on him! He had the paintings on the pulpit obliterated, and also some medieval paintings – of two churches, two kings, and two queens – in the choir. The pulpit was restored at a later date, but the other paintings were lost for ever.

Above Bykle, high on the hillside, approached by a rough track, is Huldreheimen, which means 'Witches' Home', a collection of ancient Setesdal cottages that were gathered there by the famous actor, Tore Segelke, and his wife as their summer retreat. From it a wonderful view sweeps down to the valley far below where Bykle church stands like one of its own white roses. After Tore Segelke's death, his widow gave Huldreheimen to the nation, and it is a delightful spot to visit, bypassed by so many tourists unaware of its existence.

In spite of its name, which brings to mind the fearsome *huldre* of many legends, there is nothing here to suggest their presence. A huldre can enchant Christian men with her beauty until they see her long, hideous tail showing beneath her skirt or happen to offend her so that she immediately turns into an ugly old crone before their eyes. Surely here at this Huldreheimen only those fortunate huldre who lose their tails and their evil ways through marriage in church have ever wandered in and out of these charming, black-timbered buildings that hug the sloping ground.

The turf roofs are low enough to see how the ancient craft of turfing has been carried out. First on the wooden roof there is an overlapping layer of silver birch bark, which has been removed from the trees and allowed to dry out all winter. (All farmers used to keep a stack of it, and this dried bark is still used as an 'instant firelighter' in stoves and open hearths.) Then comes the thick layer of turf, which is cut neatly and placed on the bark grass-side down, where it settles to make a weather-proof protection as cosy as thatch. Soon the rich brown covering starts to sprout new grass and flowers, catching seeds dropped by the birds and blown by the wind. In the old days it was customary to let the goats up on the roof to crop the grass when it grew too long.

The road leaves Bykle behind and climbs up to the mountain plateau where Setesdal meets Telemark and the wild reindeer roam. In Telemark is Seljord, one of the loveliest districts in the whole county; it has featured in many legends and been praised in countless songs and ballads. The small municipal centre of Seljord, at the head of a wide lake, is a good place from which to explore the surrounding countryside. The church is said to have been built at the orders of Saint Olav himself, and the saint's height can be judged by the head of hewn stone set there to mark it at the main porch.

In the churchyard a white stone monument in relief, standing almost 20 feet high, has been raised to the memory of Norway's famous travelling priest and writer of hymns, Magnus Brostrup Landstad (1802–80), showing him on horseback, looking heaven-wards, hymn book in hand. A quotation from one of his hymns is inscribed on the monument, a cry of praise that springs from the man's great wonder at the beauty of the wild countryside that he travelled so extensively.

Also close to the church is a large round boulder that has been set permanently on a base of pebbles. It bears a plaque, which states: 'This stone, weighing 570 kilos [over half a ton], was lifted by Sterke Nils [Strong Nils], 1722–1800.' Not only has this re-markable feat been splendidly acknowledged, but the little log house of this Seljord strong man – who it is said was suckled on mare's milk – has been brought down from the mountainside where he lived and now stands by a path amid the trees near by. But you have to look for it: unfortunately many minor sights of interest in Norway are not well marked at all, but with plenty of local guide literature it is fairly easy to locate whatever you wish to see. But there will be no chance of seeing Strong Nils's boulder lifted again in Seljord. Other strong men have wanted to try, but permission has always been refused. Perhaps as it is such a good story – and it has the ring of Strong Nils's own explanation for his extraordinary strength, given with a twinkle in the eye – it is best to leave the power-giving properties of mare's milk unchallenged.

Telemark is a county of precipitous gorges, vast stretches of mountain moorland, and majestic peaks that include the 6,200-feet Mount Gausta with its breath-taking, all-round view that in the startlingly clear air of the north embraces nearly one-sixth of Norway. Rjukan is an industrial town, lying hemmed in between sharply rising, forest-covered slopes. It was made famous by the daring raid in 1943 on the German-controlled heavy water factory by nine Norwegian commandos who blew it up and put it out of action for many valuable months. The film, *Heroes of Telemark*, was made here, telling the story of this feat of extreme courage. Much earlier the great Rjukan waterfall and the magnificence of the surrounding mountains had been a source of inspiration to Jules Verne.

Not far from Notodden, the industrial town that lies terraced above Lake Heddalsvann, a picturesque setting for the production of ferro-silicium, silico-manganate and plastics, lies the largest and most spectacular of all Norway's stave churches. This is Heddal Stave Church, built in the 1240s with tier after tier of dragon-headed rooflets rising from the ambulatory to cross-topped spires; it is dedicated to the Virgin Mary. Its ancient brown timbers and the primitive simplicity of its interior contrast sharply with the ornate rococo interior of the large church in Kongsberg with its sculptured gold-tasselled draperies, trumpeting angels, and the waterfall glitter of its chandeliers. Kongsberg was, until 1957, a silver-mining town, and the mines, four miles from the centre, can be visited; even on the hottest day though it is advisable to put on plenty of warm clothes before the miniature railway carries you nearly two miles into the mountain. The silver was officially discovered in 1623 by a young boy when one of the cows he was tending rubbed its horn against a stone, knocking off the moss and revealing the silver. Previously local farmers had dug silver, but had kept it quiet, for by law it all belonged to the crown.

That royal town-planner, Christian iv, came hotfoot from Denmark when he heard of the discovery to supervise the building of the town that bears his choice of a name – King's Mountain. On a mountain wall are carved the initials of all the kings who have visited Kongsberg, the most recent being those of Norway's present king.

One of the most peaceful and interesting trips to take in Telemark is on the steamer *Victoria*, which sails along an ancient waterway of lakes and canals with 18 locks through forest and farmland from Skien, birthplace of Ibsen, to Dalen, a little village at the head of beautiful Lake Bandak, where the mountains rise vertically from the water. Skien is one of Norway's oldest towns, the capital of the county, a busy industrial centre and proud of its links with Ibsen. He, however, never liked Skien, always associating it with his unhappy childhood, and having left it to become an apothecary's assistant at Grimstad he severed all close ties with the town.

Yet in a small park stands his statue, looking fiercely towards the street that bears his name. When he was still a small child his father's financial difficulties caused the family to move to their country home at Venstrøp, a few miles away, and there the house still stands exactly as it was when the young Ibsen ran home from school along the dusty lane. All around lies the softly undulating countryside, and the same peace prevails. It is a disappointment to the curators of Venstrøp that so few people come to visit the house. The window in the side porch is where Ibsen first exercised his dramatic talent, putting on puppet plays for his young school friends. To climb up the stairs into the huge shadowy loft with its mysterious corners is to get a new understanding of how it must have played on Ibsen's imagination, resulting in his using it years later in *The Wild Duck*.

In Skien itself, standing in the large Brekke Park, is the gracefully porticoed Manor House that holds many relics from Ibsen's past. Here are the reconstructed rooms from his Christiania residence with the great man's own furniture and possessions, including the simple bed and bedroom in which he died in May 1906. The two famous portraits that Ibsen painted of his brothers as a fox and a monkey hang on the walls, together with other examples of the artistic ability which he inherited from his mother.

Overshadowing even its connections with Ibsen is Telemark's unique fame as the cradle of skiing. This is the county that made skiing the sport that it is today, due in no small measure to a Telemark man, Sondre Nordheim, who in 1850 devised a new style of ski-binding, simple enough in the shape of back-fastenings stretching from the toe-band round the foot which gave freedom of movement to the heel, and at the same time put an end to the old disadvantage of losing a ski at an inopportune moment, as well as being ideally suited to the special techniques of skiing in which Telemark folk had long excelled. Sondre Nordheim was one of the greatest skiers of the nineteenth century; even as a young boy he had made history in an exceptionally long jump, which he had accomplished by putting up snow-covered planks from the roof of his hillside home to the slope behind, and then setting off to jump not only the farmhouse, but to continue on over the roof of his father's barn to land far down the hill. Slalom races had been taking place for centuries in Telemark, and it was the character-istic sharp turn at the end of the course that became known to the world as the Telemark turn.

10. Ski Land

The snow in Norway falls in time for Christmas. It has to fall three times before it stays; then the white blanket that covers the mountain peaks spreads out over the whole land. A new kind of silence descends, and the Northern Lights move like shimmering coloured silk across the sky. Tall birch wands set at the side of country roads guide the snow-ploughs that are ever on the move keeping the roads open – even a number of mountain routes that used to be closed until the snow melted. On other, less important mountain roads a barrier is lowered to show that there is no way through. Winter tyres, powerful car-heaters and getaway starting ensure that the motorist drives to work as usual. Trains and buses run on time and get businessmen, office workers and schoolchildren to work at 8.30 a.m. A business day ends at 4 p.m. – the children start home at 2.30 after only the briefest of lunch-breaks. The dryness of the climate means that light, warm clothing keeps the cold out, and if you kick the snow you see it rise in a flurry of rice-like grains. In December Oslo has a mean temperature of $-3°$ C, falling to -4 in January and February and rising to zero in March.

From early December the Christmas trees – always hung with white lights – appear in the streets of towns and villages, giving off an almost ethereal glow in the snow. A particularly tall one is set up in the forecourt of Oslo University, and as the holiday season draws near every Norwegian ship and fishing boat – sailing in home waters or far afield – will have a Christmas tree on its mast. American-style designs have recently captured the Christmas card market, but fortunately it is still possible to send and to receive the old Norwegian postcard-type. These have pictures of the *Julenisse* (Christmas gnomes in scarlet caps with white beards), snowy farmsteads with horses, sleighs and brightly feathered winter birds (such as the great tit and the blue tit) that perch like coloured baubles on the snowy trees and feast on the sheaf of corn saved for them from the summer harvest and set up outside every farmhouse on Christmas Eve. This custom of giving not only the birds but every animal on the farm a special titbit on Christmas Eve (the cows often get salted herring, which they like!) originates from the old belief that 'they were in the stable too'.

The Christmas cards usually show the *Julenisse* tucking into the plateful of *rømmegrøt* that is left out on farm doorsteps on Christmas Eve to ensure his good temper, so that he will not play tricks on the family throughout the year. He usually eats until the buttons burst off his waistcoat and he falls asleep in an old shoe, or somebody's hat.

At noon on Christmas Eve all shops and offices shut; the church bells start to ring at 5 p.m. On the west coast the traditional dish for the Christmas feast that evening is lamb, dried and salted as it was in Viking times, and served hot and steaming in golden bubbles on a bed of birch twigs. In the eastern part of the country roast pork is traditional. *Lutefisk* is often served as well, prepared since ancient times by a three-week process that includes soaking the dried fish in lye of hardwood ashes and water so that it has an almost jelly-like texture when finally cooked and served. After dinner the whole family joins hands and sings carols around the Christmas tree, though small white electric 'candles' have replaced the wax ones that I was lucky enough to see during my first Christmas at Øvstedal farm. Then comes the giving of gifts. Christmas Day is another family day and on the second day of Christmas the parties begin.

The hotels, like the more expensive restaurants, have a special *Julebord* (Christmas table) loaded with traditional fare such as smoked salmon, roast duckling and pork stuffed with prunes and apples. Sleigh-rides are arranged, sometimes with reindeer in the shafts which speed along with that unique dancing lope, the plushy surface of their antlers catching the silvery moonlight. There is skiing by the glow of spluttering torches, the flares drifting like pennants, and the arrival of the *Julenisse* with gifts for all. Many towns and villages have their own individual customs; at Kristiansand for example on Christmas Eve the ancient Oddenes Church is surrounded by a carpet of lighted candles shining in the snow.

Norwegian children, always brightly clad, even their school rucksacks a vivid scarlet, blue or plaid on their backs, are at their most colourful in winter, either zipping past on skis, or skating on the frozen lakes. Mountain lakes often freeze some time before the snow comes, and the ice, in spite of its thickness, is so clear that it is possible to look through at the water far below, sometimes catching a glimpse of a fish swimming by. Occasionally the ice groans when the water is still freezing, which can be quite eerie; it happened once when Ibsen was travelling across ice in a sleigh, and he was so frightened, always being nervous of physical danger, that he jumped out and ran to the bank.

Fishing through the ice can be a chilly, but enjoyable experience. After the snow has been cleared away a hole is drilled by a special bore – this can be a laborious task, for the ice may be four feet thick. But seated on reindeer skins, the special rod suspended over the deep hole where the bait lies far out of sight, there is the extraordinary feeling of being encased by the great silence of the surrounding countryside; the trees are huge inverted cones of snow, and occasionally huge flakes come floating down in the still air to make you as much part of the scene as any snowman. It is amazing how innocently the fish bite, unalerted by the unusual glimmer of daylight that has penetrated their dark world under the ice.

And there is daylight, for the sun does not stay away from Norway nearly as long as some people seem to think. Even in January Oslo has eight hours of daylight, and in February the skiers are already turning their faces to the sun as they acquire that honey-dark tan that by April has made them completely rust-coloured. Visiting skiers, trying the snows of Norway for the first time, are always amazed at the vastness of virgin slopes that spread out on all sides. No hard-packed surface scored over and over again, but every kind of hill and curve and angle for the experienced enthusiast and tentative beginner alike.

Easter is the time of the greatest trek of all to the mountains. Up in Finnmark the Lapps hold reindeer and sleigh races across the sun-sparkling white stretch of the tundra, and Easter Sunday sees them off to church, a straggling procession, vividly scarlet and blue, making their way along the snow-gouged path. In the Lofoten Islands the hundreds of fishing-boats are busy on their icy quest, and the coastal steamers' reduced winter fares give round-voyage passengers the chance to see the Arctic in its full icy magnificence.

In many resorts the ski season is from December to March, and the choice of accommodation is wide, ranging from the luxurious high mountain hotels to farmhouse accommodation and simple *pensionats*. Nobody is left out in the skiing season. Toddlers get skis on their feet as soon as they can keep upright and age is no barrier, many wiry old people setting off for the slopes with everybody else. There are excellent facilities for the blind, and a sighted guide ensures that they are able to take part in cross-country and racing contests.

Snorre, the chronicler, wrote of the Vikings' skill on skis, and down through the centuries have come stories of many daring feats. A cross-country race in which over a thousand skiers take part annually is over the route of the long trek made around 1200 by two 'Birchlegs', warriors so-called because they wrapped birch bark around their legs, who carried to safety the infant king, Håkon Hakonssøn, all the way from Gudbrandsdal to Østerdal and then to Trondheim.

But the event of the season is at Holmenkollen in March when the great white jump is surrounded on all sides by a vast sea of spectators, who gather from all over the country to watch their own countrymen compete with the other leading skiers of the world. This most sophisticated of sports has come a long way since the man at Rødøy travelled on his primitive skis over 4,000 years ago. Rightly it has been said that the furrow made by the plough-share, the frothy wake left by a ship and the tracks of skis all run together through the history of Norway.

Index